'Reading *Shining like Stars* is an incredible faith tonic! It felt like I was reading a modern day book of Acts. The pages are brimming with remarkable stories of what God can do with people who are willing to risk persecution and trials because they are convinced of the gospel's truth and transforming power. Lindsay Brown's insights into evangelism strategies are invaluable, not just for student work but for the whole church. He offers an exciting picture of what God is doing globally. I couldn't put the book down!'
Rebecca Manley-Pippert
Author of Out of the Salt-Shaker

'Out of the box, visionary and faith-building.'
George Verwer
Founder, Operation Mobilisation

'Lindsay Brown has shown what it means to be God's servants in today's world. His writing is based firmly on the Scriptures and illustrated with amazingly inspiring stories from the lives of students. Your heart will be warmed, your mind informed and your will challenged to involvement in God's mission.

At a time when many evangelicals who emphasize social responsibility and the need to engage the culture do not proactively go in search of the lost in evangelism and vice versa, it is heartening and instructive to see models of complete faithfulness to the full mission of the church.'
Ajith Fernando
Director, Sri Lanka Youth for Christ

'No work is more strategic than student ministry in the spread of the gospel, and no man better qualified than Lindsay Brown to tell some of the stories of its remarkable recent growth worldwide. Here is a book that informs, inspires and instructs. I warmly commend it.'
Vaughan Roberts
Conference speaker and author of God's Big Picture

'Not till Glory will we know in full how God has chosen to use student ministry to birth, deepen and extend his church around the world. Lindsay Brown's book is a faith-enriching glimpse into that story and the part that IFES has played in it. Vignettes from the past, riveting tales from the present and precious principles – all these highlight the grace of God towards and through IFES movements. Read the story – and give thanks to the Lord!'
Rose Dowsett
Vice-chairman of the World Evangelical Alliance Mission Commission

'Student ministry in the IFES family is an awe-inspiring witness to the reality and faithfulness of God. If not for the power of the gospel of Jesus Christ, the stories between these covers could not have happened. We are greatly indebted to Lindsay Brown for documenting them. Countless key Christians in national and global church leadership, in the public square and in the market place – all nurtured in their days on campus – point to the great reality of a movement of the Holy Spirit.'
The Most Revd Dr John Chew
Primate of the Province of the Anglican Church of South East Asia and Bishop of Singapore
President, Fellowship of Evangelical Students, Singapore

'God has often used universities to bring the gospel to a whole society. Richard Johnson (Cambridge graduate) brought it to Sydney as the chaplain on the first fleet in 1788. In the 1930s Howard Guinness (London graduate) inspired students to form Evangelical Unions in all the universities, and since then the essence and growth of evangelicalism in Australia's church has been inseparable from the growth and development of what is now AFES. In this captivating book, Lindsay Brown introduces us to the inspirational lives of countless university men and women, without ever losing sight of the fact that the real hero is our Lord Jesus Christ. To him be the glory.'
Richard Chin
National Director, Australian Fellowship of Evangelical Students, a founding member of IFES

(ivp)

Lindsay Brown

Shining Like Stars

The power of the gospel
in the world's universities

to Sharon

with appreciation for your hard work

and partnership in the gospel.

Lindsay

INTER-VARSITY PRESS
Norton Street, Nottingham NG7 3HR, England
Email: ivp@ivpbooks.com
Website: www.ivpbooks.com

First published 2006

British Library Cataloguing in Publication Data
A catalogue record for this book is available from the British Library.

ISBN-10: 1–84474–167–2
ISBN-13: 978–1–84474–167–0

Set in Dante 10.5/13pt
Typeset in Great Britain by CRB Associates, Reepham Norfolk
Printed and bound by Creative Print and Design (Wales), Ebbw Vale

*Inter-Varsity Press publishes Christian books that are true to the Bible and that
communicate the gospel, develop discipleship and strengthen the church for its
mission in the world.*

*Inter-Varsity Press is closely linked with the Universities and Colleges Christian
Fellowship, a student movement connecting Christian Unions in universities and
colleges throughout Great Britain, and a member movement of the International
Fellowship of Evangelical Students. Website: www.uccf.org.uk*

Dedication

This book is dedicated to all my fellow workers in the International Fellowship of Evangelical Students whose lives have been consumed with a passion to declare God's glory amongst students in all the nations of the world. It has been my privilege for twenty-five years to work and serve alongside them.

The university is a clear-cut fulcrum with which to move the world. The church can render no greater service, both to itself and to the cause of the gospel, than to try to recapture the universities for Christ. More potently than by any other means, change the university and you change the world.

(Charles Habib Malik, former President of the UN General Assembly, Pascal Lectures, 1981)

Contents

The International Fellowship of Evangelical Students (IFES) was founded in 1947 by leaders of evangelical student movements in ten countries. They covenanted on behalf of their students and staff to work and pray to see a witness to Christ among students in all nations. We now have national movements in 150 countries. Our commitment to the task is still strong as we press on to pioneer in the remaining nations.

We are equipping each generation of students to be (i) effective evangelists; (ii) serious disciples; (iii) mission-minded Christians. We want our graduates to help strengthen the world church, and to bring the presence of Christ into their professions, family life and society.

The primary theatre of our activity is the world's universities, but many IFES national movements also work in colleges of higher and further education and in high schools, so our opportunities for the gospel are very wide. The stories in this book are drawn from the university sector.

www.ifesworld.org

Preface

'shining like stars in the universe as you hold out the word of life'
(Philippians 2:15–16)

What a beautiful and rich image Paul uses of the Christians in
Philippi. He is full of aspiration for them. It is no surprise that staff
workers around the world keep turning back to his letters, for
principles and for encouragement in their own itinerant ministry.

The world's universities offer tough resistance to the gospel. It
is costly for students to 'hold out the word of life', as you will see
from this book. Yet there is no more critical sphere of influence for
the name of Christ to be known.

Student ministry is always fragile: our most experienced leaders
are Christians of only a few years standing, and thousands come to
faith after arriving at university. Yet they lead groups which are
often far bigger than an average church, right at the cutting edge of
dialogue with other faiths, and in an environment which breeds
deep antipathy towards truth. They need our prayer.

Since the fall of the Berlin Wall in 1989 we have witnessed
astonishing church growth, which is also evident in the expansion
of evangelical student groups. In 1989 the International Fellowship
of Evangelical Students had a presence in 100 countries. By 2006
this had grown to 150 countries. Behind these statistics are stories
of the way God has used students and graduates: stories which
bear comparison with any of his work across the generations.

Eric Hobsbawn in his book *The Age of Extremes* refers to the loss of a sense of history as 'one of the most eerie phenomena of the late twentieth century'. Our progressive disconnection from family and cultural roots has given rise to a profound sense of dislocation. We live in an age consumed by a quest for identity, and much of the debate is a clear product of an absence of history. This has serious implications for us as Christians. The Scriptures are full of stories of God's acts in history. Without an awareness of them, our lives can become very shallow.

By learning more of the history of the church, we see more of God's character, we understand our roots and we have our faith strengthened for action. My prayer is that as you read these stories of many educated but humble believers, you will see God's sovereign hand at work through the courageous acts of his people. May you be emboldened by them to go and bear witness for Christ wherever you are: in high school, university or in the workplace; living in a nominal Christian culture or in a culture which is hostile to the gospel.

> Therefore, since we are surrounded by such a great cloud of witnesses, let us throw off everything that hinders and the sin that so easily entangles, and let us run with perseverance the race marked out for us. Let us fix our eyes on Jesus, the author and perfecter of our faith, who for the joy set before him endured the cross, scorning its shame, and sat down at the right hand of the throne of God. (Hebrews 12:1–2)

I am especially grateful to God for the support of four Associate General Secretaries over my sixteen years in leadership of IFES: Joshua Wathanga, Koichi Ohtawa, Las Newman and Jonathan Lamb; and for the Executive Committee Chairmen: Anfin Skaaheim, Barney Ford and Dieter Brepohl. Daniel Bourdanné, my brother and fellow worker whom you will meet in Chapter 3, has been appointed to succeed me as fourth General Secretary of the Fellowship. I commend him to you for your prayers.

In telling these accounts I have been immeasurably assisted by the administrative and secretarial skills of Sophie Van Houtryve, Lindsey Capper and Kirsty Thorburn. Julia Cameron has been an indefatigable editor. Any errors of judgment or substance in the text are mine and not hers.

Lindsay Brown
September 2006

Foreword

Indigenous mission in a digital age

A quarter of a century ago, specialists in theology and mission endlessly talked and wrote about contextualization. A century before that the buzzword was 'indigeneity': the aim of mission, we were told, was to plant churches that were 'indigenous', that is self-governing, self-financing and self-propagating. What 'contextualization' added to this mix was (to coin a word) self-theologizing. In other words, Christians needed to think through the Bible for themselves, within their own language and culture, within their own contexts.

Inevitably, the call for contextualization resulted in both good things and bad things. Where the local context becomes the final control, historical rootedness – and even the Bible itself – may become domesticated. In the name of Christianity, some forms of contextualized theology became mere excuses for an array of current social agendas with only marginal connection to the gospel of Jesus Christ. On the other hand, to have Rwandans and Singaporeans and Japanese and Bolivians thinking through the Bible for themselves, learning from the history of the church, while nevertheless learning to be faithful and learning to read the Bible in their *own* contexts, was surely a good thing.

The work of contextualization must go on, of course; the need is perennial. Yet there is a sense in which the word itself sounds vaguely old-fashioned today. A lot of observers and theorists now speak of the *globalizing* of mission and of the *globalizing* of theology. In this world of rapid travel and digital communication, ideas, eye-witness accounts, stories, pictures and other bits of data travel faster than ever before. So as soon as it becomes digitally connected, no community is any longer an isolated community in which everything must be *contextualized*. For it has become part of the global community: here we learn from each other, we influence one another. Contextualization cannot be ignored, but it now lives in tension with globalization.

There are both advantages and dangers to these developments. Those who always conceive of the glass as half empty see only the dangers; those who prefer to think of the glass as half full trumpet the opportunities.[1]

Those of us who love to remember that around the throne of God on the last day will be men and women from every language and tribe and people and nation cannot help but rejoice that world mission is less and less about westerners going elsewhere to serve Christ, but about believers from everywhere going everywhere. Even in the realm of theology, while we must never, not even for a second, side-step the unique role of Scripture as the 'norming norm' for Christians, we are learning from one another, and teaching one another.

The book you hold in your hand does not address these topics in a theoretical way. It does something more foundational: it introduces you to the stories of Christians in one remarkably worldwide movement. The International Fellowship of Evangelical Students (IFES), made up of many national bodies, works in one of the most strategic populations in the world. University and college students become not only the next generation of leaders in most countries of the world, but the next generation of Christian leaders. In these accounts, Lindsay Brown opens our eyes to what is going on in the world: he helps us become 'global Christians'.

Read these chapters, and you will wonder, you will reflect, you will laugh, you will weep. Above all, you will be reminded that the Lord Christ has not yet finished calling people to himself; that we Christians have brothers and sisters in many, many places, all of them with their own stories; that faithfulness to the gospel and to the Lord, issuing in perseverance, courage and sometimes martyrdom, is still a distinguishing mark of blood-bought human beings; that all of us, not least those of us in the West, have many lessons to learn from the global church. This book is not written to address all the theological and strategic questions that might be raised, but it introduces us to real brothers and sisters in Christ, and that is important, for neither Christian truth nor Christian love can long survive if we forget there are people out there. Please, read it, and pass it on.

D. A. Carson
Trinity Evangelical Divinity School
Trinity International University

Introduction: A passion for Christ's glory

This is a book about students around the world and how God has used them. It gives just a tiny glimpse of their commitment to Christ, which for many has been at great cost. Above personal ambition has come their desire to see Christ glorified in their own lives, in their universities and in their nations. These students have taken to heart the Lord's words in the parable of the rich fool and have chosen to be 'rich towards God' (Luke 12:21); hundreds, perhaps thousands, have been faithful even to the point of death.[1]

It is their passion for Christ's glory which has driven me to write; a passion which has often rebuked and deeply inspired me. If you are a student, let these stories of fellow students spur you on in your own witness on campus. You are part of a worldwide fellowship. For all of us, may we allow the lives of these students to awaken in us again that passion we once had for Christ if it has started to wane.

Jesus Christ and the university

There are many passages in Scripture to which student leaders and staff turn over and over again. One of them is Colossians 2:2–3 where Paul is writing of his prayer for the Laodicean Christians and for others whom he has not met personally:

> My purpose is that they may be encouraged in heart and united in love, so that they may have the full riches of complete understanding, in order that they may know the mystery of God, namely, Christ, in whom are hidden all the treasures of wisdom and knowledge.

The one 'in whom are hidden all the treasures of wisdom and knowledge' – what a description of the Lord Jesus! How can we not be jealous for his name in the world's seats of learning? It is a scandal – and surely the deepest of ironies – that he should be ignored, scorned or held in derision in the very places where knowledge and wisdom are deemed to be sought and taught.

The university is the seedbed of ideas and of relationships.

The university is the seedbed of ideas and of relationships, the two critical axes of human development. It is the hothouse in which both are nurtured, for good and for ill, and, because of this, it is a critical battleground for ideologies. That is why we must work and pray tirelessly for Christ's honour here. It is no surprise that Charles Malik, the Lebanese Christian who served as President of the UN General Assembly, posed as a refrain through his masterly 1981 Pascal lectures the question, 'What Does Jesus Christ Think of the University?'[2]

If we have a strong grasp of the Lord Jesus as the agent of creation and as the one 'in whom all things hold together',[3] then we need have no fear of learning. For increasing in our knowledge and understanding of the world is a way of expanding our view of Christ.

In our discipling of students, the staff of IFES national movements encourage them to love God 'with all their hearts, their souls their minds and their strength'.[4] This full-blooded commitment is calling for ever-greater courage, as will become clearer through the pages of this book.

We are all aware of sexual immorality on Western campuses and of the pressures on students to compromise in the area of sexuality. It is less widely known that women students in Latin America and Africa are often required to sleep with their lecturers to secure a pass grade in examinations. Given the high incidence of AIDS in these continents, the tragedy is deeply alarming, for the students, for their families and for the whole culture. You will read stories here from students who have had to make hard choices.

Sharing our faith: Muslims and Christians

In the West, Christian mission is the domain of the church or of voluntary organizations; in the Muslim world, where there is no separation of religion and state, Islamic mission (*da'wa*) plays a strategic role in foreign policy.

It is no secret that money from the Gulf has been used to endow chairs in Islamic studies in several major Western universities. The Arab states have also funded core facilities like libraries and dorms as well as business schools. These facilities have been greatly appreciated by students of all religions and ethnic groups. The Muslim world is investing shrewdly to bring influence in academia – and through academia to whole nations. Within Africa and Asia, the most able Muslim students are receiving scholarships to study outside their countries. The purpose is clear – to build a new generation of leading Muslim thinkers, east and west, north and south, who will influence their countries.

So how are *we* investing? We do not have the multi-million dollar funding available to the Islamic world for mission, and in some places our labours can seem very insignificant. We worship a humble Christ who entrusts the message of reconciliation on campus to his students. As Paul puts it so strikingly in 2 Corinthians 5:20, 'We are therefore Christ's ambassadors, as though God were making his appeal through us.' Koichi Ohtawa, who served first with the Japanese movement KGK, and then with IFES in East Asia for many years, borrowed the metaphor of piling from construction engineering when he spoke of student ministry. It is gradual; it is energy-consuming and labour-intensive; it is unspectacular; and it is unseen. But it provides a vital and solid foundation for the building. Over my thirty years in student ministry I have been moved at how God has provided fine staff for this work of piling, gifted graduates who had the right perspective. You will read of several here.

God is using students in some of the most extreme situations to bring peace and hope to their nations. They have no money, but the riches of Christ; they have no human power, but the power of the Holy Spirit. They have the life of Christ in them and a gospel of hope to offer.

These students are the new generation of IFES. In 1947 when the Fellowship was formed, its ten founding members covenanted to work and pray to see a clear evangelical witness established in every university in the world. That covenant has been shared by each new national movement; it is a commitment to Christ and to one another.

Postscript

God's work in the world's universities did not start with IFES! He is the sovereign God of time and eternity, and he has guarded a witness to himself through every generation. It keeps us humble to recall our own debt of gratitude to those who kept the faith and passed it down to us. So we start the story a little nearer its beginning.

1 : Never underestimate what students can do

There is nothing so short as the Christian's memory.
(Martin Luther)

Why history matters

Martin Luther could see even in the sixteenth century just how little regard Christians had for history. We can imagine how he would respond to Henry Ford's comment that 'history is bunk', so loved and quoted today. History is full of lessons for all of us. Fashions and trends will always come and go; these are ephemeral. But nothing has changed in human nature since Genesis 3.

I remember once visiting the student movement in Israel. I was being shown around a museum with a student who was obviously not interested in history. I asked him if he had visited the museum before. 'No,' he said, 'I think history is pointless. We should only be concerned about the present and the future.' I was surprised, as we were visiting the museum of the Holocaust!

Many Christian students and graduates around the world might agree with that student, yet I believe all Christians should be interested in history. After all, the Bible is an historical book. Many times over in the Old Testament, the Jews were told to *remember* God's acts. In the book of Hebrews we have a long roll call of great men and women of faith in past history who were an example. Perhaps one of the most striking passages in the Old Testament touching on the importance of history is Joshua 4:1–7 (my italics):

> When the whole nation had finished crossing the Jordan, the LORD said to Joshua, 'Choose twelve men from among the people, one from each tribe, and tell them to take up twelve stones from the middle of the Jordan from right where the priests stood and to carry them over with you and put them down at the place where you stay tonight.'
>
> So Joshua called together the twelve men he had appointed from the Israelites, one from each tribe, and said to them, 'Go over before the ark of the LORD your God into the middle of the Jordan. Each of you is to take up a stone on his shoulder, according to the number of the tribes of the Israelites, to serve as a sign among you. In the future, when your children ask you, "What do these stones mean?" tell them that the flow of the Jordan was cut off before the ark of the covenant of the LORD. When it crossed the Jordan, the waters of the Jordan were cut off. *These stones are to be a memorial to the people of Israel forever.*'

History was important in Jewish tradition. Peter shows this when he says, 'I think it is right to refresh your memory' (2 Peter 1:13). What is the value of historical perspective? Let me suggest three important lessons.

First, history reminds us of what God has done in the past – of significant answers to prayer, evidences of his supernatural power, and the way he has intervened. This always leads to a spirit of praise. In the Psalms, time and time again the exhortation to praise the Lord came after a reminder of God's acts in history. The psalmist constantly refrains, '*Remember* how God led us out of Egypt, *remember* how he led us through the wilderness, *remember* how he led us across the Jordan, *remember* how he led us into the promised land. Therefore praise the Lord.' An historical awareness is central to a spirit of praise. The phrase 'Praise the Lord' comes 550 times in the Bible. It is the most common command and almost always an exhortation rather than an exclamation. So if you want to cultivate the spirit of praise in your church or your student group, remind people of God's acts in history. Without historical perspective, our worship will be shallow and less than fully biblical.

Second, history reminds us of who we are – our identity and our roots. Seeing ourselves as God's servants in a long line of history keeps us humble. Christian leaders who are proud often have little sense of those who have gone before, of having the baton handed down the generations to them. Humble Christian leaders see themselves in a line of saints from time past.

One of the best marks of a work of God is that it continues to grow after the leader is taken out of the way. To grasp that fact, you need to know some Christian history. If you don't read of God's work and the people he has used, you will have an insufficiently clear sense of your own heritage.

Third, we need history as we formulate a vision for the future. When we are reminded of the great things God has done, the daring attempts people have made to serve him and audacious acts of testimony, it gives us fresh determination. We see that if God has used fragile, broken and dysfunctional people, he can use us. This can give us a solid foundation from which to dream.

Beware of people who say, 'You talk too much about the past.' We should not dwell on the past, but we must start from a reminder of what God has done. May faith and hope arise in your heart as you read of his acts among students around the world.

Students in a tough arena

The earliest recorded student fellowship was made up of four international students in the country of one of the world's great powers. Daniel and his three friends were forcibly displaced from Israel and taken captive in what was the most powerful nation on earth, ancient Babylon, in today's Iraq, in the fifth century BC.

> In the third year of the reign of Jehoiakim king of Judah, Nebuchadnezzar king of Babylon came to Jerusalem and besieged it. And the Lord delivered Jehoiakim king of Judah into his hand, along with some of the articles from the temple of God. These he carried off to the temple of his god in Babylonia and put in the treasure-house of his god.
>
> Then the king ordered Ashpenaz, chief of his court officials, to bring in some of the Israelites from the royal family and the nobility – young men without any physical defect, handsome, showing aptitude for every kind of learning, well informed, quick to understand, and qualified to serve in the king's palace. He was to teach them the language and literature of the Babylonians. The king assigned them a daily amount of food and wine from the king's table. They were to be trained for three years, and after that they were to enter the king's service.
>
> Among these were some from Judah: Daniel, Hananiah, Mishael and Azariah. The chief official gave them new names: to Daniel, the name Belteshazzar; to Hananiah, Shadrach; to Mishael, Meshach; and to Azariah, Abednego (Daniel 1:1–8).

They faced a double humiliation. Not only were they taken away from their home country, but they were forced to study the language and literature of the Babylonians, their conquerors. Despite immense cultural pressure to conform, they stayed true to the beliefs which had formed their early lives; that was radical discipleship.

The story of Daniel, Shadrach, Meshach and Abednego was repeated in the early 1990s in Sudan, when the Muslim government in the north forcibly closed the main university in Juba, the southern capital, and relocated all its students north to Khartoum, in the Islamic heartland. Among those displaced were evangelical students who took the gospel with them. They courageously shared their faith with students in Khartoum and this led to an explosion of growth in the evangelical student movement. Just like Daniel they were forced to live under an alien law, the Islamic law of *Sharia*, and compelled to learn a foreign language, Arabic. It was a double humiliation for them, as it had been for him.

Like Daniel and his friends, they did not ask, 'Why has God allowed this to happen to us?' but posed the more radical question, 'How does God want me to live and speak in my new situation so that the gospel of Christ can be advanced?' That is always the question the mature Christian asks in times of trial. Just as we learn from the story of Daniel, we can learn from these humble students scattering the seed of the gospel in their own new and alien land.

They formed Bible study groups to which they invited Sudanese friends. Large numbers began to turn to the Lord. By the late 1990s over 1,300 students and graduates were coming to their annual Easter conferences. They had wider influence, too, outside the student world. At one conference, an army general from the south, the national director of an oil company and students' parents were also present. Many came to faith.

In 2001 Sudanese Christian students held a conference on world mission, hoping for six hundred participants. The venue was an Islamic youth centre in Khartoum. Did six hundred come? No. More than twice that number poured in! From the first meal, two students had to share each bowl of food. By the last day, it was three students to a bowl! Around a hundred students at that conference resolved to serve Christ cross-culturally when they graduated. This was wonderful in itself. But a further one hundred students professed faith in him over those few days! The Holy Spirit had drawn students to a conference on world mission even though they were not yet Christians – and this in a country where risks are high for those engaged in evangelism or who turn to Christ. Such news was 'more than we could ask or imagine'.[1]

The influence of students through the centuries

There is a strong case for arguing that the Reformation, one of the greatest periods in church history, grew out of a work of the Holy Spirit amongst students in Europe – that it was essentially a university movement.

Martin Luther, who had such a transforming impact in Europe and subsequently on the Western world, was converted in 1517 as a young professor of theology in the University of Wittenberg, Germany, through discovering the great doctrine of justification by faith. His first disciples were his students. Many historians argue that the Reformation took root and flourished in Germany because of the support of the German princes, but in reality the ideas put forward by Luther in his ninety-five theses were spread across Europe by students who heard and were captivated by this great message in key university centres.

The Reformation was essentially a university movement.

On the eve of the English Reformation, Thomas Ridley gathered a group of men from Cambridge University in the White Horse Inn to read from the New Testament and the works of Luther in secret. Some of this group were later burnt at the stake, including Cranmer, Latimer and Ridley in Oxford in 1555–56. Latimer's extraordinary words of courage have travelled down the centuries, 'Play the man, Master Ridley. We shall this day light such a torch as shall never be put out.' This testimony in the midst of flames has echoes of the testimony of Shadrach, Meshach and Abednego.

We know very little of the testimony of the Reformer, John Calvin (1509–64), but in his *Institutes of the Christian Religion* we learn that he was converted as a student in Orleans University, France.

Student groups appeared sporadically in different countries across Europe in this era. The first traceable instance in which students had a part in promoting world outreach was found in

Germany in the early seventeenth century. Several law students from Lübeck, while studying together in Paris, committed themselves to cross-cultural mission.[2] Three sailed for Africa. All trace has been lost of two of them but the name of Peter Heiling has survived. After spending two years in Egypt, he travelled to Ethiopia in 1634 where he spent twenty years, translating the Bible into Amharic. He died there as a martyr. Heiling had no successors and there was no continuation of what he began. It is moving to think of this group of young students banding together to pray and work for the extension of the church overseas.

Count Nicolas Ludwig Von Zinzendorf (1700–1760), who studied as a jurist in Wittenberg, was deeply influenced by his godfather, the leading pietist Philipp Spener, and by August Hermann Francke (1663–1727), founder of the Paedagogium in Halle. From an early age he was a single-minded devotee and follower of the Lord Jesus Christ. 'I have but one passion . . . 'tis he, 'tis only he,' he wrote.[3]

Together with five others Von Zinzendorf formed 'The Order of the Grain of Mustard Seed' which had very similar objectives to IFES. They highlighted their purposes as having a desire to bear witness to Christ; a desire to take the gospel overseas; a passion for drawing Christians together; and the hope that they might be able to help suffering believers. In 1732 they sent their first missionaries to the Caribbean, to the small island of St Thomas. Thus one could argue that the modern worldwide missionary movement was actually born in the hearts of a group of students who prayed together at Halle.

Converging influences

We see God's hand of providence in wonderful ways as we trace the converging of influences over the next century. The story of Von Zinzendorf's group became known in Oxford, and was an inspiration to John and Charles Wesley, founders of the Methodist movement, and their friend George Whitefield who was to spearhead the eighteenth-century revival. But there was another strand of influence on those Oxford men, which came from the north of Scotland.

The earliest recorded student-led Christian Union in modern history was founded by Henry Scougal (1650–1678) in Aberdeen University. He was evidently a highly gifted scholar and was appointed Professor of Philosophy at the age of nineteen, taking up the most senior university chair as Professor of Divinity aged twenty-three. The little book he wrote at the age of twenty-six entitled *The Life of God in the Soul of Man* was put into the Wesleys' hands by their mother.[4] They lent it to George Whitefield and through it he discovered the gospel of grace for which he had been searching. Bound into the early editions was the constitution of the Aberdeen student group, and the Wesleys used this as a model for what became known as the 'Holy Club' where they met to study classics and the New Testament.

Charles Wesley entered Christ Church College in 1726, from which his brother John had just graduated. John Wesley returned as a teaching fellow to Lincoln College, Oxford. In October 1735 the two brothers travelled to the colony of Georgia to take the Christian message to the indigenous Indian population. John Wesley's journal at the time indicates that he was not yet sure of his salvation and that his sailing for Georgia was partly a quest for knowing God better. After a disappointing period of service in the colonies, he returned to England, where he met with Christ in a worship service in London. As he listened to the introduction to Luther's explanation of Romans 1, he felt that his 'heart was strangely warmed'. And so began fifty years of astonishingly fruitful ministry. Charles became perhaps the greatest hymn writer in the English language.

Students in Cambridge

Charles Simeon came to know Christ as a first-year student at King's College, Cambridge in 1779.[5] Following his graduation, he became vicar of Holy Trinity Church. His ministry there spanned over fifty years and his wider influence proved immense. He would invite students to his rooms in King's, where he lived all his life, hosting student Bible studies, prayer meetings and evangelistic tea parties. Under Simeon's influence a group of five students formed the Jesus Lane Sunday School to reach out to boys and girls in the community with the gospel of Christ. Among them were men who were to become known for their biblical scholarship in later years, including B. F. Westcott.

Henry Martyn, a maths student who professed faith in Christ in 1800, became Simeon's curate. Martyn was the university's senior wrangler (top mathematician of his year). His decision to sail to India and to translate Scripture into Hindustani, Persian and Urdu came as no surprise to those who knew him and who could see how the glory of Christ had gripped him. But to others it was a shock that a student of such striking ability should 'waste his life' in this way. He died aged twenty-nine.[6]

In 1882, five years after the Cambridge Inter-Collegiate Christian Union (CICCU) was founded, students invited the American evangelist D. L. Moody to visit Cambridge. This was their first major attempt to

Senior friends felt it was rash.

engage the whole university with the gospel. Senior friends felt it was rash. Moody was neither British, nor middle-class, nor a university man. They were right but, as Oliver Barclay, second General Secretary of the British movement, said, 'It was rash, but it was also of God.' The first meeting drew 1,700 students. Many had come 'to have some fun'. They sang rowdy songs, built a pyramid of chairs, and responded to prayers with 'hear! hear!' Moody returned to his hotel, took off a collar that was dripping with sweat and remarked, 'I guess I have no hankering after that crowd again.' But as the meetings continued, students began to be converted. On the last night, over half of the university's undergraduates were present. Moody asked for all those who had received a blessing during the week to rise to their feet – and 200 stood. A senior friend heard Moody whisper under his breath, 'My God, this is enough to live for.' The mission caused a national sensation.

Two years later the group, soon to be known simply as 'the Cambridge Seven', offered themselves for service with the China Inland Mission – all talented men from privileged homes and all seven had long ministries overseas. They included C. T. Studd, the England cricketer, who was probably the most brilliant all-rounder in England at the time.[7] Stanley Smith, another of the seven, set off with 'a Bible and a toothbrush' to address crowded meetings throughout the country. Two thousand students gathered at Edinburgh to hear him speak, and many were converted that night. Discussion went on so late that at midnight they had to be turned out of the hall.[8]

In February 1885, the seven sailed for China, to be followed by scores of students who, under their influence, had given themselves to Jesus Christ to reach other parts of the world. Their inspiration shook the student world. CICCU senior friend Handley Moule, Principal of Ridley Hall Theological College, had to plead with his students not to forget entirely the needs of the work in their own country.

The next years were years of signal blessing, characterized by open ardent courage and passionate fervour of devotion to Christ. A tradition developed of praying earnestly to get friends to services and then talking with them personally afterwards. A Morning Watch Union was set up whose members determined to set aside at least twenty minutes each morning and, if possible, an hour for prayer and Bible study – the 'quiet time' as it is more generally known today.

Howard Guinness sets a trend

The Guinness name is well known around the world for its brewing of beer. There were two other strands of endeavour in this remarkable family line: banking and world mission. It was one of the Guinness family who set a pattern for IFES which has continued down the generations and right across the world.

Howard Guinness, a medical student, was President of the Christian Union in London University from 1926 to 1928, the year in which the first conference of the newly-formed UK Inter-Varsity Fellowship was held. Seeing the strategic value of establishing a witness to Christ in every university in Britain, the London students' eyes of faith were lifted higher. 'Could we not have an Inter-Varsity Fellowship in other countries?' they asked. The idea sparked their imagination and they sold their sports equipment to send Howard Guinness to Canada as their envoy. He sailed from Southampton with a one-way ticket and a new overcoat for the Canadian winter. Landing in Montreal, he set to work. Having established a movement in Canada, he urged the Canadians to pioneer groups in the USA. The first InterVarsity/USA group was planted in Michigan in 1938. Meanwhile Guinness had sailed to Australia and New Zealand in 1930 to found student movements there.

Through the vision and action of that group of London students, a pattern was laid. Staff and students in established movements would from now on take responsibility for pioneering national movements in other countries.

This practice has had wide implications. From early on, IFES was forging ahead as a fellowship of indigenous national movements, planting other indigenous movements. It has drawn students into cross-cultural mission with no formal theological training and without needing to learn the English language. Pioneers have come from some of the poorest countries in the world. For example, during the twenty years of civil war in Chad its displaced students, sent by the government to study in other countries, founded IFES movements in Niger, Mali, Côte d'Ivoire, Senegal and Burkina Faso. Perhaps 50% of all missionaries from India over the last fifty years have been nurtured in the Indian IFES movement.[9] If you look at the mission history in India or Chad, the stories are as outstanding as stories we read from the lives of C. T. Studd or Hudson Taylor. Nobody writes about them and yet they are some of the greatest missiological stories of the twentieth century. You will gain insights into them through these pages. It is staggering to think how these people have contributed to the cause of the gospel across Africa and Asia.

The contribution to the world church has been outstanding from national student movements in the UK, North America, Korea, Australia and New Zealand. But when the books are opened we will also learn the lesser-known stories like those of Chad and India; of Ukrainian students in Central Asia; of Balkan students in Islamic Europe; of Sudanese students and Nigerian students in the Islamic strongholds of their countries.

One student in North America

It was an unusual and prophetic work of the Holy Spirit.

The Church in North America is one of the strongest missionary-sending churches in the world. Its missionary endeavour can be traced back, under God, to one student, Samuel Mills. His mother had dedicated him from birth 'to the service of God as a missionary', which is astonishing when we realize that he was born in 1783, before any Protestant missionaries from North America had been sent out. She had not been inspired by any cross-cultural missionaries that she knew. It was an unusual and prophetic work of the Holy Spirit in that mother's heart.

As Samuel Mills grew up he was deeply impressed by William Carey's writing with its profound challenge to the church to reach the whole world for Christ. From his first week as a student at Williams College, Massachusetts, it was his custom to spend Wednesday and Saturday afternoons in prayer for the world on the banks of the Hoosack River – and he gathered four others to join him. In August 1806, he and his friends were caught in a thunderstorm on their way back to college, and sought refuge under a haystack in Sloane Field. Here Mills urged them to pray not for the world, but for themselves and for their own part in overseas mission. To bring the gospel to every culture was achievable with God's help. Remembering Caleb's words when he and Joshua returned from Canaan (see Numbers 13:30) he told his friends, 'We can do this if we will.' So that afternoon this handful of students sitting in their wet clothes committed themselves and their futures to the cause of the gospel.[10]

Mills went on to Yale to complete his graduate studies, and to found another missions prayer fellowship. The Yale group included Adoniram Judson who would sail for South Asia with a group of others on 19 February 1812: the first ever Protestant missionaries from North America.[11] Their covenant to pray for world mission led to the founding of the Student Volunteer Movement that would surge through student fellowships, sending tens of thousands into world mission. It was a remarkable work of God. (See below for lessons we can learn from its sharp growth and its decline.)

The true lifeblood of the SVM in North America is now incorporated into the aims of the IFES movements in the USA and Canada. These movements have jointly hosted a major missions convention every three years since 1947. This now takes place in St Louis, Missouri, but retains the name 'Urbana' from its earlier home in the University of Illinois, Champaign-Urbana. It draws 25,000 students. Hundreds of missionaries on every continent trace their call to serve Christ back to their time there.

Today: a whole new generation of pioneers

Since 1989, IFES has pioneered movements in fifty new countries with God's help. How have we done this with so few staff? Much has been achieved by recent graduates giving one or two years, working as part of a team.

What can we learn from the rise and fall of the Student Volunteer Movement?

The membership card of the Student Volunteer Movement (SVM) bore the motto:

'Evangelization of the world in this generation'

and the words:

'It is my purpose, if God commit, to become a foreign missionary.'

Its growth in three decades was nothing short of phenomenal. The efforts on campuses, four-yearly conventions, literature and speaking tours brought thousands of students volunteering for overseas service. By 1945, less than sixty years after its formation in 1888, at least 20,500 students who had signed the declaration sailed overseas, for the most part under the missionary societies and boards of the churches, and a further 80,000 stayed at home, pledging to support them. The motivations were genuine, the grounding in biblical principles was solid, and the leadership under the dynamic John R. Mott had a burning vision for world evangelism.

Leaders travelled extensively. Luther Wishard toured more than fifteen countries from 1886 to 1888 including Japan. The Japanese students held a national conference under the theme 'Christian Students United for World Conquest' and cabled a greeting to the American student conference:

Kyoto, July 5 1889. Make Jesus King. (signed 500 students)

That cable was read out to student leaders in Denmark, Sweden and Norway, where student groups had started meeting for Bible study, prayer and missionary concern as a result of the evangelical awakening of the 1880s. Scandinavian student conferences began the following summer with SVM movements forming in the 1890s in Denmark, France, Switzerland, India, Germany and Scandinavia. In 1895 the World Student Christian Federation (WSCF) came into being with John Mott as leader.

WSCF was a wonderful work of God. Its spirit was almost identical with IFES today. All the leaders were evangelicals. Wherever it took root, it spread the idea of personal Bible study and a daily time with God. It saw tens of thousands of students converted. SVM brought explosive growth to the missionary movement worldwide.

Yet within twenty years of its foundation, WSCF's spirituality and gospel thrust had collapsed irretrievably and the SVM died out altogether. How did it happen?

In 1920 the executive committee was expanded from six members to thirty members. Emphasis shifted away from Bible study, evangelism and a rigorous concern for Christ's glory in the world. SVM became focused on the problems of imperialism, race relations and economic justice, all legitimate concerns for Christians, but not as ends in themselves. This change was not immediately discernible and as many as 637 graduates sailed for overseas mission service in 1921. But a grasp of Christ's unique supremacy began to weaken and the watchword fell into disuse – gradually the whole argument for foreign missions lost its force and students talked of comparative religion and of syncretism. By 1936 there was such little Bible knowledge among conference delegates that one writer suggested 'they could have been described as the mission field, not the mission force'. By 1934 the number of volunteers had declined to thirty-eight. At its fiftieth jubilee celebration, Robert Wilder, the founder of SVM 'was accorded no substantial role on the programme'.

The glory was departed.

By 1959 the SVM merged with the United Student Christian Council and the National Student Christian Federation, in due course becoming part of the University Christian Movement, which by 1969 had ceased to exist.[12]

Working in teams

Jesus gathered not only the twelve apostles, but a larger group who often travelled with him (see Luke 8:1–3 where we learn the twelve are accompanied by Mary Magdalene, Joanna, Susanna 'and many others'). The apostle Paul followed that example, sometimes apparently having over twenty men and women associated with him. Silas and Barnabas were his main co-workers, but in the last chapter of several letters (especially Romans), we see reference to others.

Although Paul received support from local churches and other Christian friends, there were times when he earned his own living while he preached the gospel.[13] He worked with Priscilla and Aquila, fellow tentmakers, giving the rest of his time to evangelism and to arguing in the synagogue on Sabbath days.[14]

Much has been achieved by recent graduates.

When team leaders are effective, their enthusiasm and example rubs off on the team, especially on younger members looking for a model on which to base their life. In Matthew 9:35 – 10:20 we read of how Jesus sent his disciples out with a particular task, told them how to complete it, and what to say, and received them back for evaluation.

The IFES impetus for graduate teams grew from an initiative in IVCF Philippines in 1975. When the graduate teams began there, Leah Genita, now Chief Executive of a development agency, was teams co-ordinator.[15] She wrote an article in the *IFES Review* describing their contribution. Staff could not cope as there were so many opportunities to pioneer in university cities outside Manila and further-flung groups desperately needed assistance. The staff approached graduates to help them and in 1975 a team of five went to Davao City in the southern Philippines. The plan was to find jobs, and give their free time to foster the work. They had gone with no promise of employment, and it took almost three months before they all found work. That same year, two new graduates arrived in Cebu, following the same model.

The rationale for sending a team is simple. With a secular job, a graduate does not have much time to spare for student ministry – at most twenty hours per week. But a team of three or four graduates could pool resources and work more strategically with the students. Team members received minimal supervision and had to depend on each other. Teams rented an apartment or house, with male and female members living in separate accommodation, and their home was their base for ministry. Having these graduate teams in the Philippines made it possible to expand across the country. Today over 200 young graduates are engaged in this team ministry, under the project name 'Into all the Islands', and the model has been adopted in many other countries.

In Europe there were already small teams in the Republic of Ireland and Belgium, but no emphasis on this kind of initiative. Through reading Leah's article some of us saw new potential for reaching major cities across the continent.

Graduate pioneers in Europe and Eurasia

In 1983 we began our first team in Paris. Three young women graduates from the UK worked together with me, as newly-appointed European Regional Secretary, and my wife Ann. In our first year we put up book tables in student refectories across the city and started student groups in fifteen centres. More students came out in the summers to help us, but soon year-long graduate teams spread across Western Europe. When the Berlin Wall fell and communism collapsed in 1989, Jonathan Lamb, my successor as European Regional Secretary, felt that a natural way of expanding eastwards was by developing more teams.

North American and European graduates contributed hugely to growth as the European map was redrawn. They learned new languages, taught English, made friends with students and formed Bible study groups. It was wonderful to see. With only limited support from experienced staff they did a great job in initial pioneering. With an eye to opportunities, they developed work swiftly in all the central European countries, Russia, Ukraine and most of the former Soviet Union. This was an historic window of opportunity.

The first conference for Ukrainian students was held in 1992 and drew forty students. Two years later nearly 400 poured into the conference from twenty-five cities, including fourteen from the small republic of Moldova. I was privileged to speak at that event. After long journeys, many students arrived late on the first evening. I was giving a series of expositions from Daniel and, as we were late in starting, I didn't read the first chapter of the book aloud. Afterwards a student came up to me and asked if I would read the text the following evening, because he said 'half of us don't have Bibles'. Then he asked: 'Who is this man Daniel? I've never heard of him,' adding, 'I know the New Testament is about Jesus, but who is the Old Testament about?' I asked how long he had been a Christian. 'Four weeks', he cheerfully replied. He had become a believer from a completely pagan background. The following day I asked in the plenary session how many students had become Christians since coming to university. Three quarters of the hall put up their hands. Of those remaining, most were not yet Christians.

This was an historic window of opportunity.

Those were wonderful days of opportunity across the former Soviet Union and the teams made it possible for us to seize them. We now have ministry in twenty cities in Russia across eight time zones from St Petersburg to Vladivostok; in the Caucasus, the Baltics, the Balkans, and with a growing presence in some of the 'stans'. Almost all these young movements are already sending out their own graduates to help with further pioneering.

One Canadian team member who has given outstanding service is Brendan, a maths graduate from Waterloo University, now in one of the 'stans'. I quote snatches from recent emails to give a flavour of the varied ministry of this young Caleb. I leave them in their original form (needed for security), so occasional phrases need interpreting:

> It was a wonderful two weeks at the Eurasia Institute.[16] I took a course on theological anthropology. It was really heavy! Being taught in Russian with English translation didn't make it any easier. Our professor was very, very smart. I also did expositional pr-ching. Really interesting to wrestle through a passage then figure out how to communicate what you found.

Brendan travelled back to –stan to lead an international summer team working among local students:

> We have forty six –stani students who are loving the English culture programme and loving the team. Each Saturday we have B discussion groups. This Sunday our leadership camp begins with fifty-seven students from three cities. I am doing two B expositions and would love your 'thoughts'. Thanks for remembering Stephen. He and Al got into a long discussion and by the end of the night he joined the family! He plays guitar and has been helping with the music. I was told he has read the whole of John's book.

Elizabeth, studying Russian at Cambridge University, has just finished her year abroad. She could have opted to teach English in a Russian school, or to take a course in one of its universities. But hearing of possibilities in Central Asia, she resolved to help graduates like Brendan. Again, emails give a flavour of her time. The additional 'x' in sensitive words is to escape electronic searches:

Our student group is doing really well. We're planning a weekend conference called 'Bxible and Life' covering grace, the Lordship of JC, quiet times and evaxngelism.

I'm looking at and pxraying through different promises in the Bxible with each of the students.

The friend I asked special pxrayer for came to our BS! We plan to meet weekly to read John. She wants to understand the Bxible but remain a Muslim. Please ask Gxod to bring her to himself! I read today that 'with man this is impossible, but with Gxod all things are possible.'

My birthday was fun. I had five cakes and three parties. They really know how to make cakes here! All I ate for two days. The coldest it's got during the day is -35C and -46C at night. BTW this -stan is the 2nd fastest-growing economy in the world!

Brendan and Elizabeth have shared not only the gospel of Christ but also themselves with –stan students and graduates who, as the Thessalonians to Paul, have become very dear to them. I wish I could write more fully of the demanding and at times dangerous work they and others have done to build a foundation for a witness to Christ across this massive continent.[17] May God give us more like them with that Caleb spirit, for with God's help 'We can certainly do it'.

Those small groups of students in previous centuries could not have realized how the Lord would use their prayers. What a legacy they left!

2 : Our sovereign God and human courage

And pray for us, too, that God may open a door for our message,
so that we may proclaim the mystery of Christ.
(Colossians 4:3)

Pray as if everything depended upon God, and work as if everything
depended upon you.
(John Wesley)

In the growth of any ministry, two factors come together: God's
sovereign work behind and through history, and the courageous
acts of faithful men and women. Both these factors can be seen in
the story of IFES.

Simply put, the sovereignty of God is his controlling power
over the nations and over the life stories of individual Christians. In
my own student days in Oxford University I remember hearing
Sergei Tarassenko, a Russian physicist, speak on God's cosmic
perspective. We tend, he said, to view events in terms of how they
affect us here and now, but God has a different perspective; he sees
how they contribute to our growth in Christ-likeness, and to the

expansion and impact of the Christian gospel, in our own nation and across the world.

Again we are reminded that the mature questions in times of difficulty relate to how we can serve God's purposes and so contribute to the cause of the gospel. We see examples of this in the Old and New Testaments.

When Joseph was reunited with his brothers who had sold him into slavery, he was able to say, 'You meant it for evil, but God meant it for good.' He saw that God had turned his enslavement in Egypt to good for the sake of the people in Israel. Since his release from prison, he had risen to the position of prime minister and now had control of food distribution. From his pre-eminent position he could provide food not only for his own family but for the people of Israel and Egypt during lean years. There was not a trace of bitterness in Joseph's voice as he spoke these words to his brothers.

Similarly we find Paul writing from his jail cell to the church in Philippi, a Roman colony in Macedonia. This young church was fearful of the future. Their leader had been put in prison and they were left alone, a ragbag group of young believers unsure they could maintain their witness. Paul reminds them of three truths in Philippians 1:

- *First*, the future of every Christian is secure. In 1:6 he promises the Philippians that 'God who has begun a good work in you will bring it to completion'. He reminds them of the presence and support of God. There are hints here of his letter to the Colossians where he wrote of Christians' lives being hidden with Christ in God (Colossians 3:1–3).
- *Second*, the future of the gospel is secure. In Philippians 1:12–17, he tells us that prison guards heard the gospel because of his imprisonment and many had been encouraged to 'speak the word of God more courageously and fearlessly'. So even though the situation appears dark, Paul sees his imprisonment in God's providence as a means of advancing the gospel.

- *Third*, his own future is secure, as he emphasizes in vv. 21–24, by those rich words 'For to me, to live is Christ and to die is gain.' He exhorts the Philippians to stand firm and not to be fearful, reminding them that suffering is part of the Christian life. 'For it has been granted to you on behalf of Christ not only to believe on him, but also to suffer for him' (v. 29).

We look briefly at the break-up of Yugoslavia in Chapter 7, but let me give a glimpse now into what is happening in Bosnia, where our emerging movement is led by a gifted and able young woman from a Muslim family, whom I shall call Elena.

Elena's story

Elena told her story at a gathering of younger leaders in Hong Kong in 2005. She was converted to Christ through a school friend to whom she wrote regularly for spiritual encouragement when they were separated in 1992 at the start of the war. Her letters fell into the hands of the police in her town, and so, as a young Christian, she was called in for questioning. Her family had not known of her conversion until the police called her in. By God's grace she remained faithful to Christ in answering questions, and her family, still struggling with the news of her conversion, rallied to her defence.

Her father told the police that what she believed wasn't their business and that he didn't want their advice on how to bring up his family; her grandfather went to the general under whom he had served, and told him that if Elena were harmed, he would hold that general personally responsible; and her brother vowed to kill anyone who harmed her. And these were all Muslims! Their home was bombed twice during the war, while all the family was there, but wonderfully no-one was injured. The Lord evidently had his hand of protection on Elena's life.

There are now around twenty students in this emerging movement in Bosnia, spread over three cities. Elena, who is still a student herself, brings them together monthly for fellowship and prayer. They may be a small movement but this does not hinder them from engaging in cross-cultural mission; already they are sending two of their number to another Muslim country each summer to help the small group of students there in evangelism. We have a gospel of hope and it burns brightly.

Rebekah's story

God sometimes works in very unusual ways. Rebekah, a student who came to one of our conferences, met with Femi Adeleye, IFES Regional Secretary. Rebekah had grown up as a fundamentalist Muslim – her father was an Imam. She had never met a Christian until God reached out to her. Her life began to change through dreams (not unusual in Muslim cultures). She dreamt of a cross stretching from her pillow into the heavens, of a great white light drawing others upward while she remained in darkness and of a large book spread before her on which was boldly written in Arabic, 'Jesus is the Son of God. Worship him!'

Her heart was so stirred that she knew she must solve this riddle.

Afraid, she kept these dreams to herself. Her heart was so stirred that she knew she must solve this riddle. She met some girls from a Christian mission school, and borrowed a New Testament from them. As she read, she realized that God had revealed truth to her about the lordship of Christ. She finally invited Jesus into her life. When she told her brothers and sisters what had happened, they considered it blasphemous and shameful to the family. When they failed in their attempts to get her to recant, they began to persecute and torture her. Eventually they plotted to kill her.

One night, her younger sister sneaked out to see if Rebekah was sleeping, so that her brothers could murder her. On approaching, a bright light blocked her path. The only direction she could go was back to her own sleeping place. She went back, terrified by the light she had seen. The next morning she warned her brothers to have nothing to do with Rebekah because she was protected by 'powerful spirits'.

Rebekah was forced to marry a fundamentalist Muslim, but she continued in her faith even though her husband often kept her under lock and key to restrict contact with Christians. Rebekah's husband was desperate for a child of his own, but she suffered three miscarriages. She frequently discussed her faith with her husband and told him that they might not have children until he submitted to Christ. In desperation he allowed her to go to church and Christian meetings. That was how she was able to attend the conference at which Femi was speaking. Having shared her story with Femi, she asked him to pray for her husband and for them to have a child. As she got up from her knees, she said, 'The next time there will be three of us to meet you: my husband, my child and myself!'

Some reading this story may be cautious in accepting that this could have been an authentic ministry of the Holy Spirit. Perhaps I can share some pointers as we seek to appreciate God's special work in this situation.

Dreams were common in the Old Testament before God's Word was written down and widely available. It was his way of graciously reaching out to people when they didn't have Scripture to read and understand for themselves. Dreams were much less common in New Testament times. In pre-literate cultures or cultures where Scripture isn't widely available, God's grace is evident in still communicating through dreams today. It is very common in Muslim cultures, especially in rural areas where there is little access to written Scriptures or to radio ministry.

Where God introduces the person of Christ through a dream, his normal pattern is to bring people in contact with Christians who can explain the gospel, or to give them access to Scripture, as happened in Rebekah's case. This seems to follow the line of Romans 10:8b–15, 17 where those who call out to God are sent someone to explain the way.

So while this story may seem sensational and unusual, it is part of God's way of fulfilling his promise that all who call to him will be heard, even if they don't initially have access to a Bible. We should rejoice that there is no-one beyond the reach of the gospel if they open their hearts to the God of the Bible. Let us thank God that we have access to Scripture, and praise him for his grace in situations like Rebekah's.

The fall of communism

One of the most striking examples of how God used political change for good came with the fall of communism in Eastern Europe and the former Soviet Union in 1989. Christians around the world had prayed for this for decades, but few believed in their hearts that it could take place so dramatically.

Many Christians protested against totalitarian government, especially in Hungary and Poland. Before 1989 it was very difficult to think about starting student ministry in most parts of the communist world. A small movement had begun in Poland and Yugoslavia, and a group existed undercover in Hungary, but it was virtually impossible to penetrate the universities in Russia or in neighbouring countries such as Bulgaria, Czechoslovakia and Romania. Today we see student ministries in all of these countries, largely led by able and gifted young nationals.

One influential contributor to the birth of student work in Russia and the Ukraine was Dan Harrison, a graduate of Cornell University. He was a man of driving ambition and with a passionate concern for evangelism. In 1987 he joined Intervarsity/USA as

Associate Director of Intervarsity Missions, becoming Director of the Urbana Missions Convention from 1993. He had earlier worked with Wycliffe Bible Translators in Papua New Guinea. His dynamism and zeal made it possible for us to buy up new opportunities in Russia, Ukraine and some of the Russian satellite countries. In the summer of 1990, he arranged for short-term teams to go to Ukraine and Kazakhstan, to offer English language programmes to students over a period of eight weeks. It was a visionary move. Through these teams, Ukrainian and Kazakh students came to faith in Christ. Some team members, so excited about the openness to the gospel, stayed on to build the work. Dan died from a brain tumour in 2003.

In the Ukraine there are now established student fellowships of the new CCX movement in fifteen cities drawing some 2,000 students. During the Orange Revolution of 2004, these students set up a tent in what became 'tent city' in Kiev, where protesters could come to pray for their country. They gave out hot drinks and warm clothes; they opened their office as extra sleeping accommodation to students who had travelled from other parts of the country. The whole nation, newly-emerging from Soviet rule, was asking questions about justice and hope. Christian students were able to give a reason for the hope they had found. Vlad Devakov reflects:

The whole nation was asking questions about justice and hope.

> These historic days will be analyzed and evaluated for years, but will the new-found honesty last? This takes my thoughts away from the protesters and back to my church, and my work among students in CCX. Many of us in CCX ran to the squares to join in the protests, while taking opportunity to serve our fellow Ukrainians. It was no hardship for us. People needed warm socks and gloves; they needed shelter and food. Once the socks and soup were

provided, long Ukrainian conversations began with real needs and
fears exposed. Deep down, protesters wondered where they could
find strength to give honest weights a year from now. I wondered
too. I wondered if those who hope in the new democratic
government will 'soar on wings like eagles; run and not grow
weary, walk and not be faint'.

We still have much work to do in the Ukraine, but there is now a
gospel witness in many universities, and students are being
equipped to respond to those 'long Ukrainian conversations'. Kiev
also hosts an annual training school for graduates from across
the Eurasia Region who are now working among students. Its
courses aim to develop a solid theological foundation, a biblical
world-view and practical ministry skills.[1] Dan Harrison was a man
of vision.

Across the world God has used unsung, untrained, unknown
heroes from many countries, just like the Chadian and Sudanese
students, to take the gospel to other nations. Of course he also uses
people who have been well trained in seminary and Bible school,
but it is a fallacy to argue that it is essential for people to go
through that system before God can make use of them. The
growth of student work in central Africa, Russia, Ukraine and
neighbouring satellite countries like Kazhakstan shows this. These
pioneering graduates may have served on the committees of their
own campus groups or led small Bible studies in their universities,
but that was all the experience they had to offer.

God's sovereign plans in moving people

Another remarkable example of our sovereign God turning bad
into good was in the aftermath of the Gulf War in the early 1990s.
This war, which issued from Iraq's attempt to seize and annexe
Kuwait, brought immense suffering in Iraq. Many fled the country
to travel across the border to friendly Jordan. The trauma of those

days led to the awakening of mission awareness in the Jordanian church, and the growth of Jordanian student ministry. Many Iraqis who crossed into Jordan were welcomed into the homes of Christians living in the Jordanian capital and were stunned at the hospitality and kindness shown to them by Christians.

They naturally asked, 'Why are you being so kind to us Muslims?' One Christian told me how he replied. He said simply, 'The love of Christ has been shown to me, and I wish to share it with you.' When I visited Jordan in 2003, a local church leader told me so many Iraqis had become Christians that there were now more Iraqi Christians in Amman than Jordanian Christians. The testimony of believers in Jordan also impressed people in government. Crown Prince Hassan wrote of the contribution Christians made in the Middle East, describing those in Jordan as the glue which holds the culture together, even though they were less than 1% of the population. Under the leadership of Hussam, the first national staff worker, student ministry accelerated.

It was in part the kindness shown by Christians that led to more openings for the gospel. The Jordanian Evangelical Theological Seminary (JETS) based in Amman was opened in 1991 and has made a significant contribution to the church in the region. It now draws over 100 students at any one time on its residential bachelors and masters programmes and its graduates are serving in thirteen countries across the Arab world. Its short summer schools are having a growing influence throughout the Middle East. Beyond these is a growing programme of theological education by extension, as well as radio broadcasts going throughout the Gulf States.

In each of these instances, believers could wring their hands in despair when faced by such trials and obstacles. But with the eye of faith they were able to see God at work, breaking up the ground and creating opportunities for the advance of the gospel. As someone once said, 'Without God we cannot; without us he will not.' Our sovereign God graciously calls us to work together with him.

A telephone call from an airport

Let me share another story of God's sovereignty, and the way he uses amateurs. In the early 1990s, a group of young people from the University Presbyterian Church in Seattle were sent on a short-term programme to Belgrade. When they arrived at Frankfurt airport after their overnight flight from the US, they heard on a news bulletin that civil war had broken out in what was then Yugoslavia. They phoned their missions pastor to ask him what to do. He had seen on the news that the Albanian government had just fallen, so he suggested they go to Albania instead!

Bravely they caught the next flight to the capital Tirana where they spent four weeks, and God used them to bring ten young people to faith, who in turn would plant the IFES movement we have today. One of those ten was Zef Nikolla, a gifted linguist, who is now its national director. Zef took a year out of ministry to learn New Testament Greek thoroughly, so he could join the team translating the New Testament from the original Greek into modern-day Albanian. The translation was published in 2005. The student ministry is now active in each university in the country, and many of its graduates have taken up key positions in church leadership. That team of students could have had no idea of the way the Lord would use them over their summer vacation. We thank God for the spiritual antennae of their missions pastor. In Albania now we have a wonderful example of how investment in a generation of students benefits the life of the national church over the long haul. This is a key element in the vision God has given to us – graduates going on to build and to strengthen Christ's church in every nation.

Two international students

Now to another very different illustration of God's sovereignty at work. Derek Mutungu from Zambia came to study at Bath

Technical College in England. In the first week of term he met a few Christian students who invited him to a church service. He happily went along, hoping to find friendship, and was welcomed by a family into their home. Over a period of several weeks, Derek heard the gospel taught, and he responded to the overtures of Christ. Gifted and dynamic, he quickly grew as a Christian. He was impressed by the testimony of the Christian students in Bath and subsequently in Imperial College, London, where he went on to study for his degree. Having seen the effectiveness of Christian Unions in the UK, he returned to Zambia determined to form a similar student ministry. He became its first staff worker, supported by IFES, and quickly set about building a Christian student group in the University of Lusaka, the capital city. The work grew rapidly and in due course as many as a tenth of all the university students in the country were Christians. News spread to the then President, Kenneth Kaunda. He invited Derek Mutungu and the leader of the local student group to the palace. When they met, President Kaunda asked Derek, 'What is this message you are preaching which is turning the university upside down?'

Derek told him, and Kenneth Kaunda was moved to tears. 'This,' he said, 'is the message our culture needs to hear. Come back in two weeks and bring the other student leaders with you.' Derek and the leaders of the Christian Union returned two weeks later to the presidential palace to meet the entire Zambian cabinet. 'Now,' said Dr Kaunda, 'preach to them what you preached to me.' They did! So through the kindness shown in Bath to one student, far away from home, God was sovereignly establishing a Christian witness among students in another country and through those students the gospel message would be preached to their government.

Then there was Dika, a highly able linguist from the Democratic Republic of Congo, working towards his doctorate in Cardiff University in Wales in the 1980s. While there, he became a believer. After he finished, Dika worked alongside the small French IFES movement for a few years before returning home.

International students

One way God has worked behind the scenes is through the huge spread of international students across the world, especially since the 1960s. Their numbers run into millions, from countries such as China, Greece, India, Malaysia, France, Japan and Turkey.

They are often the crème de la crème of their societies, returning home to become leaders in academia, business, the civil service and politics. This makes a ministry amongst them very strategic in world mission. As they travel from their home countries, they leave behind their roots and expose themselves to other influences, including the possibility of gospel influences.

It is intriguing to note how few people became Christians at home in the Acts of the Apostles. Timothy seems to have been a rarity. Most were converted, from the Day of Pentecost onwards, when they were away from home. We have an obligation to care for the foreigner in our midst. See, for example, Leviticus 19:33–34: 'When an alien lives with you in your land, do not ill-treat him. The alien living with you must be treated as one of your native-born. Love him as yourself, for you were aliens in Egypt. I am the LORD your God' and Deuteronomy 10:19: 'And you are to love those who are aliens, for you yourselves were aliens in Egypt.'

IFES enjoys close links with agencies set up specifically to serve international students and to help those who become Christians to settle into a church when they return home. Most staff in these agencies have served first with the IFES national movement or been student leaders in their national movement.[2]

He then taught Linguistics in the University of Kinshasa. In the late 1980s, I received a telephone call from him. He was in New York. He told me how in the previous few weeks he had shared meals with the presidents of France and the USA. I said, 'So what are you doing these days, Dika?' He told me that soon after he returned to Congo, President Mobutu had invited him to be his translator as he travelled to events around the world. He said, 'I was in Washington and Paris travelling with my president as his translator. I believe God has placed me there so I could share the gospel with him.' Today Dika is a university professor in the Democratric Republic of Congo, and directs the ministry of Navigators in that country.

What strategic value there is in international student ministry!

Standing firm

Once captured by the glorious light of the gospel, it is our responsibility to stand firm and proclaim Christ, no matter what the cost to ourselves, as God works behind the scenes. There are innumerable examples of students and graduates who have done this. I will share just three more.

Once captured by the gospel, it is our responsibility to stand firm.

Forty years ago a student ministry quietly began to grow in Vietnam with the help of an OMF missionary, Paul Contento. It was led by Cuong, who became its first General Secretary. He skilfully developed the work in the midst of the Vietnamese war, which divided the country North and South. America backed the South in an attempt to strengthen its stand for independence against the advance of communism. That war brought tens of thousands of deaths. In 1975 the Americans withdrew and, at the last moment, Cuong was offered the chance to leave the country with some American troops. He refused, preferring to stay to be a testimony to Christ in that situation. On 1 May that year he wrote a letter to Chua Wee Hian, then General Secretary of IFES.[3]

> I decided to stay and I do not encourage any of the Christian
> students to leave the country. Their faith needs to be proved under

trial and God will not let them down if they truly believe in him. I doubt the kind of faith that is easy-going. Here they will be a witness to those who need Christ the most. My ministry will be restricted, but they will have more opportunity to witness and to uphold one another. If all desert Vietnam, who is going to be here to witness to the other side?

The letter ended poignantly, on a note of triumph:

> This is probably my last communication with IFES. Pray for me and the students, and the church in Vietnam, for wisdom to face the coming fiery trial. Our Lord has risen. We are going to suffer, to die and to be raised up with him in glory. Please extend our warm greetings to all IFES member movements. Thanks.

When he wrote that letter he was only twenty-six years of age.

Cuong planted a church, aided by students and graduates in the Vietnamese student movement. The church grew to several hundred within a few years. Because of his growing influence he was eventually imprisoned. On one occasion interrogators challenged him, 'Do you not understand what we could do to you?' His response was quick and brave. 'Do you not understand what God can do to *you*? You may be able to harm my body, but ultimately one day you will all have to stand before the judgment seat of Christ.' Soon after this interrogation, they released him from prison and expelled him from the country. Today he is still serving the Vietnamese church but outside the country.

Another outstanding example of courage and determination to speak the gospel in trying circumstances occurred in Peru in the 1990s. A guerrilla movement called *Sendero Luminoso* (Shining Path) arose, bent on bringing down the government and destroying the church. During the 1980s they systematically killed over 300 pastors and many female Christian workers simply because they were proclaiming an alternative message of hope through the redeeming gospel of Christ. A story was told of two students going to a church meeting carrying Bibles. The students were stopped by a young guerrilla who ordered them to throw the Bibles on the floor and spit on them. One student did, the other didn't. They shot the student who spat on his Bible and released the other, telling him, 'You can go free because you stood by what you believed.'

It was in this context that I visited Peru in 1992 to take part in a student conference, arriving just a week after elections had taken place. We were in Huancayo, in an area where many students had been killed only a few months previously. During the elections, two local pastors were kidnapped and the local mayor shot dead on his doorstep. It was a disturbing situation. The conference centre, just outside the city, was located close to the base for the guerrilla movement. It had not been used for over a year because of the dangerous situation. I asked the students why we were there. Typically they responded, 'Because we got a good deal – it costs only a dollar a day.' I admit I was very concerned for my own life. My only daughter had died not long before and I cried to the Lord to spare my life for my family's sake because I thought it would be too great a burden for them to lose me as well in a short space of time.

While reflecting on this, I talked with a young student, Amelia, who was studying sociology in the University in Huancayo. She asked me what I thought of studying sociology. I told her I thought it was a useful subject and asked why she inquired. She said most male students on her course were in the guerrilla movement. She had become a believer only three years earlier when the guerrilla movement was at its height. At that time student guerrillas put up a notice on campus with a list of the people they were going to kill. As they killed them, they ticked them off, one by one. She said Christians in the student group urged them to stop the killing, but they refused and said that if Christians didn't remain silent they would kill them too. When she heard this, she was frightened for her life and said nothing about her new-found faith for two years. She went on, 'Six months ago I asked myself the simple question: Is the gospel true? If it *is* true, then it is worth living for, and it is worth dying for. After several months of reflection I became convinced that the gospel was true. Since then I have spoken openly of Christ, counting the cost.'

I was rebuked by her testimony. In an age when it is fashionable to emphasize our feelings and our sensitivities, let's note what strengthened Amelia – the conviction that the gospel is true. When faced with difficulties, our feelings will naturally be wayward. Only a real conviction of the truth of the gospel will buttress us, hold us together and give us confidence to press on in living for Christ. He came to give us good news, not good feelings.

My final story comes from Burundi. I visited this country in 1994, in the midst of civil war between Hutus and Tutsis, when as many as 200,000 people had been killed. I stayed with the movement's General Secretary, Emmanuel Ndikumana, and his wife Asèle. Over breakfast I asked Asèle how she felt about Emmanuel travelling around the country. The previous day he had set out for Rwanda to meet me, but his car overturned on a mountain pass on the way. In the providence of God, Emmanuel survived. How had Asèle felt when she heard the news? 'I am always prepared for news like this,' she said. 'He goes to visit student groups every day, and I don't know if he will return home. Guerrillas are spread out all across the country, and the student world is an obvious area for attack. Emmanuel is a prominent leader, so he is likely to be a target.' At that moment we heard some crackling noises in the nearby hills. At first I thought it was the breakfast cereal! I asked her what the noise was. She said it was the noise of gunfire in the mountains. 'You will be travelling through those mountains this morning to get back to Rwanda!' Suddenly I became more deeply aware of the daily pressures that some of our staff are facing.

It is worth living for, and it is worth dying for.

Emmanuel came to the UK to complete a Masters course in 2000. He sent me an email shortly before leaving Burundi. 'Last night,' he wrote, 'we were huddled in the hallway wondering if we would make it to the UK. Fighting was raging all around us. Local believers ask, "Why don't you leave permanently while you have the chance?" But God has called me to serve here, and if I leave when others can't, it will come as a great discouragement to them.' The Ndikumanas returned to Africa with their two children. This merging of passionate love for the gospel, one's people and one's nation is attractive and truth-affirming in the life of Christian workers. In October 2005 Emmanuel and Asèle faced deep tragedy with the death of their third child, Camilla-Shalom. Here is the email they sent to the IFES family:

It is with great sadness that we inform you that our little Camilla-Shalom, the last of the Ndikumanas, passed away yesterday. She was at home with her baby sitter who was getting her ready for a bath. Leaving her near a small basin half-full of water, she entered inside the house to get some warm water to mix with the cold water. When she came back less than five minutes later, Camilla-Shalom had drowned herself in the water. The baby sitter was without first-aid drowning experience and by the time she got her to the nearest clinic about ten to fifteen minutes from our home, Shalom was no longer.

You can imagine our shock when, less than one and a half hours after we left home, we received the message telling us that Camilla-Shalom was dead! We rushed to the hospital only to realise that the bad news was actually a reality. Her baby sitter was in a terrible shock.

Camilla-Shalom had turned one year last month. She was just growing normally, very energetic and extremely awake. She was a great joy to us. Those who know where she got her two names (Camilla and Shalom) will understand our momentous perplexity. However, she is gone but we remain with the One who had given us her. He is our ultimate hope and joy. With his help and the support of all of you, we remain standing and hope to continue to look ahead and move.

She will be buried tomorrow. Your prayers will be very much appreciated. She is gone, but we remain with the One who had given us her. He is our ultimate hope and joy.

Such people shine as stars before the watching world.[4]

With a weak view of God's sovereignty, we crumble easily when difficulties come. We need to remind ourselves that he is sovereign over the passage of history, over the history of nations, and over the history of individual lives. At the same time he is gracious and good, loving his people and offering grace to strengthen us and steel us in times of trouble.

We are called to stand courageously and proclaim the gospel, because it is the great Truth which all the world needs to hear. It is this conviction that drives and undergirds the growth of the International Fellowship of Evangelical Students.

Such people shine as stars before the watching world.

Be strong and very courageous. Be careful to obey all the law my servant Moses gave you; do not turn from it to the right or to the left, that you may be successful wherever you go. Do not let this Book of the Law depart from your mouth; meditate on it day and night, so that you may be careful to do everything written in it. Then you will be prosperous and successful. Have I not commanded you? Be strong and courageous. Do not be terrified; do not be discouraged, for the LORD your God will be with you wherever you go (Joshua 1:7–9).

3 : Holding out the word of life

Evangelism is our *raison d'être*. It is the heartbeat of our movement.
(Prof. Samuel Escobar, IFES Presidential Address, 2003)

I thank all the students in this room for helping me to know Jesus.
My life has changed. He became the sun of my life.
(Sargylana, Yakutsk, Siberia)

Evangelism has been at the heart of IFES ministry from the time Stacey Woods became the founding General Secretary. He had kept it as first priority in Canada and the USA where he had served as General Secretary of both Intervarsity movements, and he appointed senior staff like David Adeney, David Bentley-Taylor, David Penman, Gottfried Osei-Mensah, David Gitari, Alistair Kennedy and John White to work with him – men who would keep it at the core of the national movements in their care.[1]

By God's grace we trust that planting the seed of the gospel and working to nurture that precious seedling of faith in students' lives will always remain central. For Jesus Christ is the Saviour of the whole world. He is the Saviour of his church in every culture: in countries given over to hedonism and materialism; in countries traumatized by ethnic cleansing and genocide; in countries emerging from communism; in the Muslim world, the Buddhist world, the Hindu world; in the tiger economies; in the fragile economies. Evangelism among students is always urgent. There is an unusual openness to the gospel in the student world, but for each new generation it lasts only for a few short years. It is moving to hear of the deep commitment of Christian students to bring the gospel to their friends.

Student creativity

Students can be very creative in their evangelism. I recall hearing about a small group of Christians in the Polish university town of Rzeszow. They were only a small group so how could they make an impression on a large university? They settled on an unusual idea to publicize an evangelistic event.

Three of them dressed up and went visiting in student dormitories, knocking on doors. As people opened the door, first came the student dressed up as 'Death', scythe in hand, announcing, 'It is appointed to men once to die, and then the judgment.' Then he ran off.

The poor students were shocked! Five minutes later, another knock came. As student after student opened their doors, they met a student dressed up as an angel. The angel asked, 'Has Death come here recently?'

'Yes,' the student would say.

'Well, I want to tell you that Jesus Christ has died and risen from the dead to conquer Death. Tomorrow night the Christian student group will explain how Christ's resurrection gives hope in the face of death.' Then the angel would run away.

Students went back into their rooms, and five minutes later a *third* knock came. This time the students found someone dressed like the devil. The devil look-alike said, 'Psst! Has an angel been here telling you about a meeting tomorrow night?'

'Yes,' would reply the student.

'Don't go. It's nonsense.'

Of course the one thing you never say to students is, 'Don't', because then they do! Hundreds went along, the meeting was overflowing, and fifteen professed faith in Christ that night.

In the University of Valdivia in Chile, students put up posters inviting people to receive a free copy of the New Testament. A giant model of the New Testament was placed at the entrance to the campus. The special week of events opened with a ceremony to which the media and the university authorities came. Animated films were shown in the university, telling the lives of different historic characters, including Jesus. Afterwards the students spoke of their faith in the resurrected and living Jesus and offered copies of the New Testament. During the week they invited a local band to play in the university canteen, and again shared the gospel, offering copies of the New Testament.

The Christian students went to clean the toilets.

In Cuzco, Peru the student group planned, prayed and worked in preparation for their evangelistic mission. The students asked if they could address the faculty of the university, but they were turned down because faculty members said, 'What can we learn from students?' So they went to the Rector of the university and asked, 'Can we serve in some way?' He said, 'The toilets are very dirty. They haven't been cleaned for a long time. Would you clean them?' So the Christian students went to clean the toilets. It took forty-eight hours, they were so dirty. News spread around the campus as they had evidently aroused the curiosity of the student body. This got back to the Rector who was so impressed by the Christian students that he sent lecturers to help them on the second day! God used the students' serving hearts to provide the meeting with faculty for which they had longed. Opportunities to testify to fellow students followed in abundance.

When the students moved on to proclaim the gospel, the blessing was extraordinary. One afternoon they carried big crosses on their shoulders, each cross with a photograph and a name of a famous character in science or history: Mao, Che Guevara, Lenin and Marx . . . The last student carried an empty cross. They paraded these around the campus and after about half an hour a huge crowd of students had gathered. Then one of the Christian students got up and said, 'You see these crosses we are carrying around the campus. On them are the paintings of four great leaders. They were great men. Now they are dead. The fifth cross is empty because that represents Jesus Christ, who died and has risen again. We want to tell you about him today.' They preached the evidence of the resurrection and dozens of students professed faith in Christ.

A mission in Guatemala City in 1992 had a special focus on first-year students. As in Costa Rica, the planning group used the context of the 500th anniversary of the arrival of Christopher Columbus. Five hundred years after Christopher Columbus arrived in the Americas, the gospel has still made relatively little impact in the university world. There was much work to be done in planning, in training, in prayer. Students put massive energy into it from January onwards and gained help from sister move-ments in Ecuador, Costa Rica, Panama, Nicaragua, El Salvador and Honduras as the new students began to arrive in March. They drew audiences of 200 attentive students a night. Through a mixture of personal conversations, public proclamation, literature, drama, films and music, almost all 17,000 first-year students in the country's national university heard something of the gospel. Over the course of the week eighty-five students professed faith. One of them wrote: 'What convinced me of my need of Jesus Christ as Saviour? The combination of Bible study and your friendship.' The students continued working hard, running a discipleship training course until December.

In Ecuador the student movement piloted a survey of the National University of Ecuador in Quito. It covered attitudes to a range of issues and the final question read: How would you respond to having Jesus Christ as your classmate? One afternoon the students went to the faculty of law, the cradle of the *avant-garde*, pervaded with a strong sense of Marxism. There was disappointment with the country's political leaders and with the leadership of the faculty. After some dialogue, the Christian students posed the question about Jesus Christ. Surely he would change many things and could give them new hope. The Christians then urged them to consider not just the historical Jesus Christ, but the Christ of faith, the Christ we read of in Hebrews.

The response was amazing. Students decided to follow Jesus straight away. Then one student told of his experience the previous night. He lay awake worrying about the country's problems and about personal decisions he had to make. With a degree of desperation he asked God to show him what he should do if he really existed. Then he fell asleep. With tears rolling down his cheeks, he said to the Christian students, 'You were sent by God so I could meet him myself.' The believers too were in tears. After praying they hugged each other and praised the Lord for the work of the Spirit and the power of the gospel.

In McMaster University in Canada in the 1990s, students held a campus mission with the British evangelist Michael Green. During that time they received permission from the Student Union to open a campus bar on the Sunday of the mission so they held their first 'Church at the Rat' worship service and then three more 'Church at the Rat' services during that year. By the last one, and with 400 students coming, they outgrew the bar. They moved the following year to the largest bar on campus, 'The Downstairs John'. The students ran the programme, staging drama and giving testimonies, and stepping in for the main speaker when need arose.

In the UK it is not uncommon for Christian Unions to draw over 1,000 students to a Christmas carol service on campus. Since 2003 the Christian Union in Exeter University has hired the city football ground and extended invitations beyond the university to the city. The local newspaper advertises the event, now an established part of the local calendar, and sends reporters to it. How did it begin? The CU had, the year before, hired the largest university venue, with a capacity of 800, half-filling the hall with 400 students. They were heartened by that number. The following August, Emma Brewster of UCCF staff received a call from Kate Harrower, a third-year law student. Emma takes up the story:

> Kate called and said, 'Emma why not go for the football stadium this year?' My thoughts were: *we haven't yet filled this venue – wonderful to dream a dream Kate, but rather ambitious. I had visions of a small number of us trying to sing carols in the rain!*
>
> Praise the Lord Kate ignored my advice and went ahead anyway. She called me later and said, 'The stadium is booked so let's get on with planning it!' Oh me of little faith – it was wonderful to see Kate's hunger to make the gospel known to the city, her perseverance in going ahead despite my nervousness, and her excitement as we planned the event with the whole CU, and drawing in local churches. The first year 2,200 came and this is now close to 3,000. It is the largest carol service held in the south-west – and perhaps in the UK?! It was inspired by a student and is run by students, and it has been an inspiration to the local churches to see what students united around the gospel can achieve.

In Egypt, Christian students were banned from using the university premises for evangelistic meetings, so on one occasion they hired a boat to take 300 of their friends on the Nile. After entertaining them with food and drink, they openly shared their faith. It is moving to see the lengths, and the expense, to which Christian students go to bring the gospel to fellow students.

In Mexico City Christian medical students were prevented from holding evangelistic Bible studies on the university campus. The only place they were offered was the morgue in the hospital. Unperturbed they accepted, and invited non-Christian friends to a

Bible study on 'Evidence for the Resurrection'! There among the dead some came to life spiritually if not physically!

Holding out the word of life to our friends

For many years, the strapline we used in IFES to describe our activity was 'students reaching students'. It reflected our ethos: staff as the enablers, students the ones on the front line. It also expressed the centrality of personal evangelism. Right through church history Christians have shared their faith with their friends. In Acts 8:4 Luke writes of how the early Christians 'gossiped the gospel' wherever they went. This highlights their great delight and joy in passing on the Christian message. The church grows fastest when people like us talk naturally and openly about our faith.

From the start our *raison d'être* has been to stimulate personal faith in the Lord Jesus Christ and to further evangelistic work amongst students throughout the world. As we look back over our own story, I would like to suggest four principal approaches, learned from the Lord Jesus himself, which have borne fruit:

- *First*, he mixed with a wide range of people. Too often Christians separate themselves and have no other friends. Jesus was known as the friend of sinners. He calls us to be morally distinct but not to be socially segregated. He himself lived out the need to be in the world, among the people he had come to save.
- *Second*, he was a good listener. We see in the Gospels how he listened to people's concerns, aspirations, needs.
- *Third*, he asked questions. This was central to his personal approach. He didn't come to each conversation with a package to be delivered or a bomb to be dropped. He asked questions. His encounter with the Samaritan woman is a clear example of this.

- *Fourth*, he had enough understanding to weigh up what he heard from others. In Luke 2:46–47 we see him taking time to listen to the religious leaders before making his own contribution. When he brought his own contribution to discussions, his hearers were amazed.

Listening, engaging, interacting, understanding, treating each individual differently and clearly explaining Christian truth were all central to Jesus' approach to evangelism. Like Jesus we need to spend time with our neighbours. We need to be clear in our understanding of the Gospels and we need to be natural in sharing with those around us.

In many student movements there has been a strong emphasis on prayer triplets. This was an idea developed by the evangelist Billy Graham, whereby he encouraged groups of three Christians to pray together regularly for three friends each – i.e. a total of nine unconverted friends. This emphasis on specific prayer for individuals has brought many blessings. When we pray for friends, not only does God hear our prayers, but we tend to be more alert to opportunities to speak to these friends when we meet with them.

They had been struck by how the Oxford students were praying for their friends.

I remember bringing a group of senior staff from the German IFES movement to a week of evangelistic activity in Oxford University when I co-ordinated IFES work across Europe. They came to see if they could learn anything from the Oxford students for their own university evangelism. I was at a meeting in Germany when they reported back. They had been particularly struck by how the Oxford students were praying for their friends specifically by name. 'We don't do that in Germany', they said. 'We tend to pray more generally that God will work in the world.' My own experience of being part of a small prayer group as an undergraduate was seeing God open up the hearts of friends to receive the gospel as we prayed specifically for them. Personal testimony, a distinctive lifestyle and specific prayer are a dynamic trio in God's hands.

Holding out the word of life through small groups

In the early church God used small groups, often gathered together in homes, as a means of engaging people with the person of Christ. We see this in Jason's home (Acts 17:5), the home of Titius Justus (Acts 18:7) and in Acts 2:6–46 where we are told there was a house full of seekers.

One of the best examples of small group work occurred in Singapore. The leaders decided to rename the fellowship groups as 'contact groups'. The students would meet three times per month for Bible study, fellowship and prayer, then on the fourth week invite friends they had been praying for throughout the month. In a context of significant local church growth and with this shift in focus, the work began to grow, expanding from 150 students to some 1,500 students over several years.

Later, other IFES pioneers such as Ada Lum and Ruth Siemens developed an approach called evangelistic Bible studies where students were encouraged to gather in small groups to look at Jesus' encounters with people in the Gospels. These groups provided an opportunity to take a more careful look at the Person and claims of Christ.

Ruth Siemens was living in Barcelona, Spain, when she met a vibrant and warm undergraduate from the American mid-West who was on her year abroad. The student's name was Becky Manley. Ruth saw the potential to be harnessed in this student's life and invited Becky to share her flat in Barcelona. Ruth had pioneered student movements in Peru and Brazil, and served among students in Portugal. Now she had come to Spain to help strengthen the ministry there. She had a deep grasp of God's sovereignty and like Ada Lum she loved to introduce students to the living Christ through the pages of his living Word.

Under Ruth's guidance, Becky found herself leading an evangelistic (or seeker) Bible study group for her friends in Barcelona. Years later, now as Becky Manley Pippert, she wrote candidly in her book *Out of the Saltshaker* of how she hoped no-one would come! That book has helped generations of students to grow in their confidence in the gospel and to introduce their friends to the Christ of the gospel. Becky Manley Pippert regarded Ruth Siemens as a mentor, and valued her friendship for the rest of Ruth's life. Ruth died as I was about to complete this chapter. I quote from Becky's affectionate tribute to her:

> When Ruth encouraged *me* to lead a Seeker Bible Study in Barcelona, I thought she'd been in the Spanish sun too long! Imagine my astonishment when every international student I invited to the study came – and soon began inviting their friends to come as well! Five students gave their lives to Christ in that study and as a result my own life was changed forever. But that was then. Does Ruth's strategy work for today's postmoderns? More than ever! In my own evangelism training ministry, people are not only learning an incarnational approach to sharing faith, but we've seen Seeker Bible Studies begun in America, Europe and Asia. And to think it all started from a single Seeker Bible Study in Barcelona at Ruth's prodding!
>
> Why was Ruth's ministry so fruitful? Because she engaged in the eternal! There is much talk today about our need to be *cutting edge*. Simone Weil, the French philosopher, wrote perceptively: 'To be always relevant, you have to say things which are eternal.' Ruth had absolute confidence that true spiritual power lay in utilizing God's supernatural resources.
>
> Does that mean our witness is removed from the perils and struggles that engulf humanity? Does *engaging in the eternal* mean we cast a blind eye to social injustice, poverty or world hunger? Absolutely not! The love of Christ demands our ministry to every

aspect of broken humanity including the care for our battered planet. But as important as it is to mediate the love of Christ – it is not enough. We must be armed with *all* of God's supernatural resources: declaring God's truth and exposing seekers to his living and written Word; depending on and being filled with God's Spirit through prayer and other means he has provided, and displaying God's love. It is important to be relevant, but what I learned by watching Ruth is that *only the eternal is eternally relevant.*

Using the gospel narrative

In my experience, students often lack confidence in the power of Scripture to convict and, with the help of the Holy Spirit, to transform lives. Students therefore need to be encouraged to expose their friends to the accounts of Matthew, Mark, Luke and John, where they can see the words of Jesus. Becky Pippert's book and her evangelism training have helped students ask good questions about their own confidence in the gospel, especially in the West.

Hundreds of thousands of students are being invited to engage with the gospel.

Let me share with you now how hundreds of thousands of students are being invited to engage with the gospel in the Middle East, Africa and South Asia.

It is a hallmark of IFES that we share ideas. UCCF, the British movement, launched 'The Big Idea' in the 1990s. The idea came to Nigel Lee, then Head of Student Ministries, suddenly in the middle of the night. Why not offer a gospel booklet, a 'biography of Jesus', to every student living in university accommodation throughout Britain and Ireland? At the time 90% of UK students had no idea what Christianity was. The student movement had little money and they were short-staffed. It would take a miracle to get this off the ground. An impossible dream? They wrote to the Bible Society with the idea and waited. Back came the offer to provide 500,000 copies of a Gospel without charge!

The plan was not simply to organize a mass distribution of a part of God's Word, though this in itself would be useful. It was to set up hundreds of evangelistic discussion groups where Christian students could explain their faith to their friends. Luke's Gospel was chosen because it had the flavour of a modern film script. In fact people could use the *Jesus* video, based on Luke's Gospel, to accompany the study and present Christ.

Another key principle was to help Christian students get to know one Gospel thoroughly, so they could use it for the rest of their lives. UCCF prepared study materials as well as evangelistic outlines. The Big Idea ran from October 1994 to Easter 1995. At least 300 students professed faith over that time. Copies of Luke's Gospel with an intriguing cover were handed personally to each student in halls of residence by door-to-door visits and through special events. In just one term more than 400 enquirer groups were set up, led by students.

In Glasgow one girl spoke to a male student in her hall of residence, who said he had thought a lot about God and began to think it might be true. She put his room down on a list of rooms 'not to be visited' as she would follow it up herself later. But the pair who went door knocking got the numbers mixed up and did visit the room by mistake. The man was overwhelmed and wanted to talk and ask questions. After much discussion, he gave his life to Christ. Prior to the Christians knocking on the door he had prayed, 'God, if you are really there, give me a sign'. He could hardly believe it when they appeared almost immediately and gave him a Gospel.

This wonderful approach was picked up by many other IFES movements. In Norway in 1997 the students gave out 50,000 copies of Luke's Gospel to friends, and launched over seventy discussion groups. As I write, some fifty student movements across Africa, the Middle East, South Asia and Eastern Europe are embarking on similar programmes with a total of 500,000 Gospels and New Testaments in over twenty local languages. In each case students are being trained to lead Bible study discussions which take their friends to the heart of the matter, looking at the Person and claims of the Lord Jesus Christ.

Why public proclamation is important

Proclamation evangelism has been used throughout the history of the church, and we must not neglect it in our student movements or churches. It was the approach of the apostles in reaching those from nominal Christian backgrounds (see Acts 2), as well as those from pagan backgrounds (see Acts 17). A lack of confidence in public proclamation arises from either a lack of confidence in God's Word, or bad experience of preaching, or both. The early church evangelists sought to understand the local culture as their starting point, but ultimately the core of the gospel was always proclaimed.

In his masterly book *Evangelism in the Early Church*, Michael Green argues that wherever the apostles started from in their preaching, they always concluded by focusing on three truths: *first*, that there is only one God who is our creator and to whom we are morally responsible; *second*, that the death and resurrection of our Lord Jesus Christ are distinctive authentications of his uniqueness; and *third*, that repentance is necessary in light of the reality of judgment to come. Some contemporary evangelism neglects one or more of these key features and is the poorer for it. I once asked Martyn Lloyd-Jones, the first Chairman of IFES, what he felt were good models of preaching. He said we should always start by seeking to satisfy the mind; then go on to speak to the conscience, leading to repentance; then challenge the will, calling for a response; inevitably the emotions will be touched. He said much preaching goes wrong because preachers either start with the mind and stop there, or go straight to the emotions and evoke rapid response based on minimal understanding. This often leads to spurious professions of faith.

The British evangelist David Watson coined an interesting phrase in an attempt to describe the kind of proclamation needed in a word-resistant culture. He used the term 'teaching evangelism'. We need to explain biblical truth and then apply it evangelistically to the hearers. For example a preacher may start with the question of suffering and why it is such an obstacle to many coming to faith. He may explain that the God of love who sees suffering in the world is not immune to it himself, having sent his only Son to die on the cross so that human beings could be delivered from all consequences of sin.

In our preaching we should explain terms such as grace, justification, repentance. We should be clear and simple, but not simplistic. Preaching needs to be thrustful, accessible, punchy and heraldic. It can be carried out to great advantage in a neutral context on campus – a lecture theatre, a hall or the college bar.

Best practice: a threefold approach

In the best student groups all three emphases of personal evangelism, small group evangelism and proclamation evangelism are used together. These three approaches complement each other. When movements use all three together, it is powerful. It avoids an over-emphasis on personal evangelism which can miss out on the importance of engaging friends with the Person of Christ – through the text of Scripture, or through heraldic preaching. Student groups can seek a quick fix by arranging big public meetings. But if the groundwork isn't done through friendships and small groups, then few people become Christians. The students then become discouraged about public preaching and give up on it. We need to engage in all three together. Perhaps they can be understood in the form of a pyramid (see figure 1).

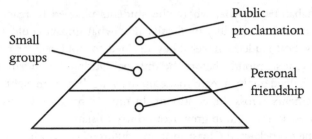

Figure 1.

The turning point for the IFES movement in Costa Rica came in 1992. They formed small groups to reach out to faculties and secondary schools so that the light of the gospel would spread widely. Personal friendships would form the base of the pyramid in their evangelism and they would seek to listen, love and reach out with compassion to their friends.

They worked to present the gospel in a way relevant to each area of study. For example, in the agronomy school, students produced a tract on the stewardship of creation and ecology. The psychology students designed a low-cost mural, alluding to struggles of individual and social conflict. After displaying the mural, they invited students in lectures to come to small group Bible studies.

At the top of the pyramid, the university group as a whole organized larger scale activities. To commemorate the 500th anniversary of the arrival of Christopher Columbus, they designed a mural contrasting the Christ of the Spaniards and the biblical Christ. This was a major project and in preparation the students gave themselves to careful reading and reflection. They hung it in the busiest part of the campus and it led to many personal conversations. It was not until after this that they arranged public proclamation, focusing on the living Christ and the liberty he brings, as opposed to the enslavement which the *conquistadors* brought.

One of the best examples of an IFES movement bringing together all these principles in one mission occurred in 1991 in

Cochabamba, Bolivia, where the students planned to reach the whole campus – faculty by faculty. But what impact could a few evangelical students have? They decided to hold regular prayer nights for six months before the mission. During the mission they were helped out by a team made up of evangelists from eight IFES movements across the continent. In time 'submarine Christians' surfaced and the group grew from thirty to sixty.

They proclaimed Christ in many different ways. Medical students came to a film and discussion about abortion. Language students were invited to a Bible translation exhibition. The team of evangelists led Bible studies in each faculty and there were open-air crowd-pullers such as pantomime, Christian music and sketchboard evangelism. During the six-week mission this small group of Christians presented the gospel to all 20,000 students on campus and hundreds professed faith in Christ. This was unprecedented.

Before that time the church had grown rapidly amongst the poor in Latin America, making little impact among the educated and middle classes. The early 1990s were a period of unique, remarkable openness to the gospel among university students. Following the Cochabamba experience came fifteen evangelistic missions in seven different countries in 1992 and 1993. Missions were run by local students with the goal of sharing the gospel with all their fellow students over several days. An evangelist was sometimes invited to these events for a special presentation, but the main tasks were organized and carried out by the students themselves.[2]

Eva Morales, General Secretary of the Bolivian movement, was a student in Cochabamba at that time. She reckons 80% of those involved in the mission are active in gospel work now among students, whether as pastors, university teachers or church members. 'The Cochabamba Mission raised the profile of the Bolivian movement significantly, both within the university and within the evangelical Church. It had a strong impact on one student generation's commitment to trans-cultural mission.'

Evangelism and the world of ideas

Our calling as a Fellowship is to establish a bridgehead for the gospel in the university world. Our major work is with under-graduate students and we equip them in every way we can to sound a clear note for Christ in this arena.

In an address to a group of IFES staff in 2006, Professor Nigel Cameron, a shrewd commentator on the university world, endorsed the critical nature of Charles Malik's question that I quoted in the Introduction: 'What does Jesus Christ think of the University?'[3] He observed that Christian students and Christian academic staff can tend to show ambivalence towards the intellectual functions of the university, even though these func-tions drive the nation's culture and its values – it is critical for the gospel to penetrate university life at this level if we are to see substantial influence for Christ in a nation.

He continued: 'This ambivalence stems partly from an older anti-intellectualism that we would now generally disown, and also from a failure to appreciate the importance of ideas in determining culture (and in setting everyone's default assump-

Evangelism and ideas go hand in hand.

tions, including those of believers). It also reveals a false dichotomy, as if conversion did not involve a radical re-orientation of our minds; so evangelism and ideas go hand in hand.' He then went on to outline three further points, all pertinent to any consideration of IFES ministry:

1. The impact of postmodernism has been over-stated, but there is no doubt that the intellectual environment is today both more challenging for Christians (in that we have lost our place as the would-be thought-leaders of the culture) and more open (people find us and our ideas less

threatening). Our apologetics is still largely tied to the idea that, in human terms, you win a convert by winning an argument. This is still true: but arguments are very different animals in a postmodern context.

2. My chief fear as I look ahead is that we shall have plenty of believers, especially in the global south and in North America, but their grasp of the implications of 'belief' will get thinner as time passes. Public culture and its assumptions will be left to the secularists, and the church will be slowly throttled as Christians live and think much like their neighbours, with a veneer of piety that gets thinner with the passage of time – and the growing secularization of the culture.

3. So how we view the university, and its role as 'a factory and marketing machine for ideas' (to borrow Malik's phrase), will finally be the litmus test of the church of the twenty-first century. The strategies we develop for the presence of the church inside the university will set the pattern for the church at large.

We must therefore:

(a) evangelize in a manner that speaks to the minds of students and teachers, and to the mind of the culture;

(b) develop strategies that build credibility for the Christian world-view within the university, for example by making common cause with secularists on matters of common concern (e.g. human rights; biotechnology and human dignity; relief of poverty, etc.), so that without diluting our distinctive convictions we show that at some key points in the contemporary agenda we agree with what many others are saying – and have our own frame of understanding in which these convictions fit;

(c) never forget that change comes about in all contexts through a combination of ideas and relationships – so we

will both engage, and encourage students to engage,
in the building of durable relationships with colleagues,
relationships that are not narrowly focused on religious
objectives but that offer a window into discipleship as
they encounter the Christian life and world-view.

These are central matters which bear on all university evangelism
and which underline the need for a thoughtful apologetic.

'Always be ready to give an *apologia*'

Apologetic evangelism can be defined as 'giving a reasoned
defence of the gospel'. In 1 Peter 3:15 the apostle encourages
believers to: 'Always be prepared to give an answer [*apologia*] to
everyone who asks you to give the reason for the hope that you
have.' As Nigel Cameron points out, this is especially important in
the university context. Some Christian students arrive at university
from an environment where they have been encouraged to *stop*
thinking and 'only believe' without asking questions, and that is a
travesty of growing up into Christ as a believing student. A clearly
reasoned presentation of the gospel acts, not as a rational
substitute, but as a basis or ground for faith; not as a replacement
for the Holy Spirit's working, but as a means by which the
objective truth of God's work can be made clear so that people
will heed it as a vehicle of the Holy Spirit. We have examples of the
apologetic approach in Scripture in Acts 17:2–3, where Paul talks
with Jews who have some biblical knowledge, and verses 16–31,
where he talks with non-Jews who have no biblical background.

Apologetic evangelism addresses the question, 'Is Christianity
rationally defensible?' It can be used to demolish apparently
rational arguments against Christianity so that the evangel can be
heard, and it is often a means of communicating the truth of
the gospel in words and terms which are understandable. It has the
useful by-product of encouraging Christians by providing biblical

answers to academic questions they may be asking themselves. Richard Cunningham, Director of UCCF, the British movement, has brought a strong emphasis on apologetics, and UCCF has a website www.bethinking.org to equip students in this arena.

Peter May, Chairman of the UCCF Trust Board, wrote a fine article on Christian apologetics in 2005 in which he concluded: 'Paul summed up the apostles' approach in his second letter to the Corinthians: "Knowing what it is to fear the Lord, we try to persuade others" (2 Corinthians 5:11). Unargued evangelism had no place on their agenda. Persuasive evangelism is the only example they have set us.'[4]

Christianity is never exclusively rational – it also has moral dimensions. We must not pander to people's intellectual curiosity, but give them a full basis for believing. Wherever we start in our apologetic approach, we must ultimately present people with two things: the objective Person and work of the Lord Jesus Christ; his deity, death and resurrection; and our own personal experience of the living Christ.

> *The Christian faith goes beyond reason, but that does not mean it is against reason.*

The Christian faith goes beyond reason, but that does not mean it is against reason. Jesus never argued against reason. In John 20:24–29 when Thomas doubted his resurrection, he made a distinction between faith and sight, not faith and reason. 'Thomas', he said, 'It is better if you have believed having not seen me' (not having not thought things through). The danger for the apologists is that they may start so far back in seeking to answer questions that they never reach the evangel. The best form of apologetics should include a reasonable defence of the gospel and lead on to a proclamation of the gospel. So the apologist should take people's questions seriously, but move on to raise the matter of truth and speak of the historical Jesus. It has become an established pattern in many week-long university missions to have apologetics speakers at lunchtimes who at the end of their question and answer sessions will invite everyone to hear the gospel proclaimed in the evenings.

'Such good news'

In Nepal, following the breakdown of the political system in 1990 and the advent of religious freedom, the student work began to grow and reached over 500 in membership. Disillusionment with traditional Hinduism, the fall of communism, and the new freedom to evangelize, gave the student movement unprecedented opportunities. Their response was an intensive campaign of distributing evangelistic literature. Student teams rose at 5am to get literature ready to distribute at the gates of the campuses as people arrived for classes. Teams also visited village schools, walking for hours carrying literature – and to one place a projector, generator and film. The teams travelled all over the country giving out literature to over 25,000 students on more than fifteen campuses. They witnessed hundreds coming to know Christ. 'I just could not resist the feeling that here is a group of thinking students who have a grip on reality which I have been searching for', was the comment of one new Christian. Another added from the heart, 'We have never received such good news before.'

The mid-1990s were challenging times in central Africa. Daniel Bourdanné, IFES Regional Secretary for Francophone Africa, visited Rwanda shortly after the civil war in which almost one million people were killed in 1994. He found a great hunger there for biblical truth, and took the opportunity to demonstrate its foundation for life. In Kigali he gave an apologetic lecture on 'Reason and Faith' to 1,000 students and teachers. The President of Rwanda heard about this and asked for a recording and it was also broadcast on national radio. Daniel was invited to the national university in Butare to give an apologetic talk on the origin of man. It drew 1,000 out of 4,000 students in the university and many faculty members, including those with no Christian faith. It made a big impact on the university. As this book goes to press, it is not unusual for 3,000 students to come to weekly meetings in that university. Not all are Christians, but they are drawn because they can see that it is the gospel which offers hope.[5]

Planning a strategy

Through this chapter I have tried to emphasize how we should work from biblical principles in university evangelism and the importance of working creatively and strategically. We urge students to play an active role in student life as we hold out the word of life – to join clubs and societies – and we encourage a good proportion of the Christian group to live in university accommodation.

It seems to me that there are five keys to developing an ongoing evangelistic presence in the university. We need:

- to analyse the issues on campus – to understand students' problems, anxieties, belief systems and interests, so the subjects they choose to tackle are helpful and relevant;
- to look strategically at the campus: for example lunch arrangements, important meeting places, and plan our meetings accordingly;
- to equip and mobilize every Christian student, to train students to know what the gospel is, how to share it, how to give a testimony and how to lead a person to Christ;
- to take initiatives in small groups in the halls of residence, departments and faculties: for example, a question panel on the authenticity of Scripture for the lawyers; a study of 'the God of the poor' for geographers and human scientists;
- to plan special efforts to reach particular groups, for example international students, postgraduate students, faculty members.

An evangelistic strategy seeks to equip and mobilize every member in the group to share the gospel with those on their course, in their corridor, in their sports team. The strongest programmes are planned with the academic year in mind. The beginning of the year is a crucial time for new students and international students. Evangelistic events can be followed by Bible studies and discussions. In short, if our attitudes and ambitions are right, and if we are prayerful and dependent on God, he will give us the good ideas and the opportunities.

4 : Students and world mission

Declare his glory among the nations,
  his marvellous deeds among all peoples.
(Psalm 96:3)

A key means of reaching whole nations and people-groups is to work through students at universities. This is one of the most strategic ways of reaching into all ethnicities in multi-ethnic countries. And where the national universities draw international students who have come to the country specifically to study before returning home, this adds a springboard dimension, as those converted to Christ can then take his gospel back with them.

When IFES was founded, the approach of mission agencies was still to send westerners to the developing world and remained so for at least another two decades, but this has never been our mindset. When Chua Wee Hian, a Chinese Singaporean, was appointed as the second IFES General Secretary in 1972, he was the first non-westerner to lead any international mission. From the start it has seemed natural to equip students and graduates from every continent for cross-cultural mission.

Student ministry has given a powerful impulse for world mission and every IFES movement is committed to it as a central focus for each campus group. The stories of Adoniram Judson, Henry Martyn and the Cambridge Seven will be in print for many years to come, but they are not alone – they represent not hundreds but *thousands* of other stories.[1] Stories of students who have been gripped by the gospel and who say with Paul, 'Christ's love compels us'.

The Urbana Missions Convention (see p. 31) is perhaps the best-known student convention in IFES. For many years it has hosted a training track for the organizers of other missions conferences around the world, making a major strategic contribution to the birth of similar conventions across Africa and Asia, and to the growth of missionary vision in these traditionally 'receiving' nations. The IFES movements in Taiwan, Korea, Brazil, Mexico, Nigeria, Kenya and India all host missions conventions regularly. Many thousands of cross-cultural workers have heard their call from God at these events. Their stories could fill a book in themselves.

Eugenio Restrepo, originally from Bogotá, Colombia, sensed God's call to cross-cultural ministry at Urbana in 1987. He says, 'God worked in my life and gave me a concern for urban ministry in Europe. So I committed myself.' He now serves in Malaga, Spain, developing training seminars for leaders and writing and performing drama sketches for street evangelism. God has used mission events like this all around the world to call students to radical commitment for the long haul. In people like Eugenio and those whose stories you are about to read, we see how he is able to keep what they have committed. He can sustain students and young graduates through lifelong decisions.

I well remember the missions conference in Nigeria in 1991 which drew 4,000 students. At the end of the conference, one of the preachers called for students to offer themselves to go on a short-term programme to the neighbouring Muslim republic of Niger to preach the gospel there. He needed fifteen people to join the team, but 1,000 came forward to offer themselves! What a sight that was. We sense that the Holy Spirit has been working in an unusual way in recent years in mobilizing students for mission.

But missionary vision has never been limited to inspirational conferences. IFES movements have always encouraged students to take the gospel to other students, from different cultures as well as from the same culture.

Mission at the heart of the gospel

'Why bother with mission?' The answer permeates the whole of the Bible. If we are uninterested in mission, we are unbiblical Christians, for our God is a missionary God. The Old Testament, the Gospels, the book of Acts, the Epistles, Revelation are all full of references to God's love for the whole world. At a time when pluralism and its first cousin relativism influence so much of our thinking, we need to be clear that mission is part of the gospel.[2]

He is a missionary God – Father, Son and Holy Spirit.

These are the objections I hear most often:

Objection 1: It's only for those who 'feel called'
All believers must be engaged in worldwide mission because of the God we worship. He is a missionary God – Father, Son and Holy Spirit – who has a missionary vision and creates a missionary church, sending it out into a needy world.

God is a missionary God
We see our first missionary, Abraham, sent out by God himself, as early as Genesis 12. Through him God promised to bless all the

families of the earth. There are many stories throughout the Old Testament of God reaching out to the Gentiles.

For example Ruth was a Moabitess (from present-day Jordan); Naaman was a Syrian; Jonah was called to reach the Gentiles of Nineveh. Psalm 96, where believers are exhorted to declare God's glory among the nations, links worship and mission, so mission is a fruit of full-orbed biblical worship. The psalmist writes of singing a new song to the Lord and then declaring his name amongst the nations. Any worship which does not express something of God's concern for a needy world is truncated, perhaps even unbiblical.

Christ is a missionary Christ

Jesus spoke of coming to rescue the lost sheep of the house of Israel, but he also reached out to Gentiles. Think, for example, of his dealings with the woman of Samaria (present-day Palestinian Territories), the people of Decapolis – ten Gentile communities beyond Galilee – and the Canaanite woman.

After his death and resurrection, Jesus commissioned his followers to go to all nations with the Good News and make disciples.

The Holy Spirit is a missionary Spirit

Often cross-cultural mission is relegated to a church committee, yet in the Acts of the apostles, the whole church was mission orientated. We hear much about the gift of tongues given to the apostles in Acts 2. The primary reason for this gift was so people could hear the gospel in their own language. The Holy Spirit came at Pentecost to help Christians fulfil their mission.

Through the book of Acts, the missionary Spirit creates a missionary people and sends them out on their missionary adventure, beginning in Jerusalem, then on to Samaria and ending in Rome, the capital of the world at that time.

Furthermore, most of the New Testament letters are sent to missionary-planted churches. To argue against engagement in mission, we would have to ignore most of the New Testament. Finally we come to the consummation of the age. Revelation looks forward to the fruits of worldwide mission. In Revelation 7:9–11 we read of people from every tongue and every nation worshipping around the throne of the Lamb of God, the Lord Jesus Christ.

The Bible is full of references to every tribe, every people, every nation and to the ends of the earth. The God of the Bible reveals himself as a missionary God. So if we truly worship this God and obey his Scriptures we must be mission-minded believers.

Objection 2: The needs of our own national church are so great. How can we give time to helping other countries?

As the church has got involved in the worldwide missionary enterprise, it has grown at home. The converse is also true.

One of the most striking examples of this is the early church in North Africa. If we look at a map of the church in the first few centuries, we see much growth in North Africa. Today the best-known church leaders around the world come from Anglo-Saxon cultures. In the first three centuries, however, most of the prominent leaders came from the Middle East, Southern Europe and North Africa, for example Augustine of Hippo, Athanasius from Egypt, Origen of Alexandria and Paul of Tarsus (in present-day Turkey). The early church in the Middle East and North Africa was vibrant.

With the exception of a large church in Egypt, there are only a few thousand believers now across North Africa in Libya, Tunisia, Algeria, Morocco and Turkey. What happened? In the early centuries these Christians fought for the primacy of biblical truth – we owe a great debt of gratitude to Athanasius for his defense of the doctrine of the deity of Christ in the third century. But over the generations the arguments moved to secondary issues, as ardour for the central truths was gradually lost. By the sixth century churches focused on form rather than content, and, when Islam reached North Africa following the death of Mohammed, it swept through the region in one generation – that region has been captive to the influence of Islam ever since.

By contrast, if we look at the European Reformation in the sixteenth century, we see a concern for truth which was allied to a concern for proclamation and for taking the gospel across cultures. The architects of the Reformation did not see much beyond Europe, but as believers were persecuted and converged on centres like Geneva where John Calvin taught, they were so captivated by the truth claims of the gospel that they spread out all across Western and Central Europe, influenced by the writings and teachings of Calvin, Luther and others. It was with this spirit that the famous Scottish preacher John Knox returned home from Geneva in the 1550s, 'refreshed by springs from the fountain head'.[3] Gripped by the truth, he determined to proclaim it in Scotland.

In the famous church in Wittenberg where Luther pinned his ninety-five theses at the birth of the Reformation, there are stained-glass windows of Reformers from all across Europe, including Finland, Sweden and Hungary, who, influenced by the new teaching, proclaimed it throughout Europe.

Gripped by the truth, he determined to proclaim it.

There is a famous story told of Oswald Smith, pastor of the People's Church in Toronto. When he arrived there as a young preacher, the church was on the verge of closing down. On his first Sunday he preached twice on mission. At the mid-week church prayer meeting attended by only a few people he spoke about mission. Eventually one of the elderly ladies plucked up courage to speak to him: 'Mr Smith,' she said, 'You are preaching about the need to take the gospel to the ends of the earth. But our church is on the verge of closing its doors because we are so few.'

He replied, 'Sister, if we do not have enough conviction to desire to proclaim this message to the ends of the earth, our church will die.' As the church grew, they began to support missionaries and today their membership is several thousand strong, supporting several hundred missionaries.

History demonstrates that as the church has been involved in the worldwide missionary enterprise, so it has grown at home. If we want to see our national church at home strengthened, paradoxically we must develop our missionary vision.

Objection 3: The gospel has been proclaimed to most of the world. We should call a halt on cross-cultural missions

It is true that the evangelical church has grown enormously in the last 150 years. There are an estimated 13,000 ethno-linguistic people groups in the world. At least 9,000 have a viable Christian witness, the vast majority reached in the past forty years. In 1810 few churches existed outside Europe, north-east America, South Asia and Cape Province in southern Africa. Today the church is global, with more than 300 million evangelicals and many millions more who claim to be followers of Christ.[4]

Nevertheless, an urgent effort is now required in the majority world to ground national Christians in their faith, especially in areas where growth has happened so quickly. Preachers must be equipped to handle Scripture well, and we need able graduates with a depth of theological understanding to teach in seminaries. Christian writers and Bible commentators also play critical roles – those who will interpret Scripture for their own culture and context, so the church 'self-theologizes' (to borrow Don Carson's phrase) in a manner which is robustly biblical.[5]

Great needs for evangelism still remain. Some 4,000 ethnic groups have no viable Christian witness says world mission statistician, David Barrett. There are 4,300 languages still with no Scriptures. These represent lost opportunities to reach people in their 'heart languages'. Evangelistic activity is distributed very unevenly worldwide. At least one fifth of the world has never heard the name of Jesus. We argue about his second coming when a billion people have not yet heard of his first coming. Where are our priorities? There is a role for all of us in fulfilling the Great Commission to make disciples of all nations.

It was a passion for world mission which drove the early leaders of IFES, sensing God's leading to build an indigenous, evangelical student ministry in every country where universities existed. When the work began in 1947, movements existed in ten countries. Today that work has spread to 150 countries. But there are at least eighteen more countries with tertiary education where we do not know of any established witness to Christ in their universities.

As mission is at the heart of the gospel, it must always remain at the heart of teaching programmes in student groups. What distinctive contribution do students bring to world mission while they are still students? God uses amateurs! Yes, they make mistakes that older and more experienced Christians will not make. But they are the best-placed evangelists in our universities. It is students who do the work of reaching students, of planting the seed of the gospel in these seats of influence in nations.

God uses amateurs:
from everywhere to everywhere

Many have given their lives for this quest.

Students are young and less bound by the traditions of their parents' generation. In situations where ethnic tensions run high, they can powerfully incarnate the message of forgiveness and reconciliation. Many have, in fact, given their lives for this quest, as we see from stories in this book.

Students are also more highly mobile. Let me give two illustrations from the Caribbean of this flexibility and mobility. By 1996, students in Martinique and Guadeloupe had been praying for French Guiana for seven years. The Lord seemed to be urging them to go there, but how would they raise the money? Where would they stay? What would they do when they got there? There was then no way of flying there from Martinique or Guadeloupe.

But that summer a new airline was set up, though it stayed in business just a few months.

A French Guianan graduate from Martinique arranged for a team of students to be hosted by Christian families in the capital city, Cayenne. Their visit would last two weeks. What diversity they found! Creoles, descendants of slaves; bush Negroes; Amerindians; Chinese; Hmong who came from Laos during the Vietnam war; Europeans and immigrants from Brazil, Suriname, Haiti and the West Indies. Such contrasting lifestyles: from Amazonian Amerindians at one end to Europeans working in the space agency in Kourou, where the Ariane rockets are launched. IFES ministry was not known at all, so the students needed both to inform Christians, and to provide training. They met with pastors, church leaders, youth workers and, of course, other students. They used Scripture to help show the need for student mission – and prepared maps, pictures and brochures to display and hand out. They also accepted an invitation to speak on the local radio station. In Cayenne and Kourou they ran one-day training sessions for potential supporters and for students, showing how students could be equipped to run a group on their own campus.

Later that year the first group began in a high school in Kourou – then others appeared. Soon Marc Pulvar was appointed as IFES staff for the French-speaking territories in the Caribbean and he began to make regular visits to French Guiana. Now, several years later, the work is still expanding, bringing the gospel to all ethnic groups. Though from different worlds, all are educated together, and this provides a unique opportunity to reach many people groups.

In Francophone Africa, Chadian students and graduates have made an enormous contribution to the expansion of the gospel in the last fifty years. According to the United Nations this landlocked country is one of the poorest in the world. The Chadian student movement, Union des Jeunes Chrétiens (UJC), began in 1957 in the midst of a civil war which continued for several decades. Thousands of students had to leave the country to further their studies. As Christian students moved out to enrol in universities in other parts of Africa, they carried the gospel with them. Through this dispersion, God used them to pioneer IFES student movements in Côte d'Ivoire, Mali, Guinea, Senegal, Niger, Burkina Faso, Morocco and Tunisia.

Daniel Bourdanné was one of those students. He left Chad in 1980 to study in Togo then in Côte d'Ivoire just as student ministry was in its early stages. After Daniel graduated, he was invited by Solomon Andria, IFES pioneer staff, to be Travelling Secretary for six West African countries and later to develop literature ministry throughout West Africa.[6] God used Daniel to help build student movements in the Republic of Niger, Guinea, Senegal, Mali and Burkina Faso. During this time he met his wife Halymah, a student in Niger. Daniel is a world authority on millipedes – one of the more unusual routes into long-term student work! In 2004 he was invited to play a role in the political arena in his country and his sharp, perceptive mind combined with his gentle manner would have fitted him well for this; but that perceptive insight also traced the active hand of God in the university world, and Daniel resolved to continue serving in IFES.

God saw our tears and opened the door of the interior.

Barka Kamnadj, another Chadian and a good friend of Daniel, worked to pioneer a student movement in Guinea, West Africa. There was a core of only a handful of Christian students in the capital Conakry when he arrived in 1993 and the ground had not been well prepared. This small group was uneasy about his coming and even wrote two open letters against Barka and his wife and distributed them widely. At the University of Conakry everything had been put under lock and key so that it was impossible to work. It was a tough start, but over the next five years he trained up two national staff to take over from him.

He writes, 'God saw our tears and opened the door of the interior outside the capital where there was no organized student ministry.' A medical doctor helped them plan their first missionary journey. They began by starting cell groups in the interior city of Macenta which developed quickly. As the work picked up speed, Barka was able to appoint his first three staffworkers, all fruit of that missionary visit to Macenta. By 1998 he left behind a thriving work led by nationals, with 500 students in groups across the country. He then moved on to Niger Republic, which is 98% Muslim, and from there to build on Daniel's work in Burkina Faso.

Barka continues, 'A simple life of conforming to Christ by God's grace can make a difference. This is what we learned in Guinea, and we proved it again in Niger and in Burkina Faso. One of God's beautiful gifts to us over the hardest time is our children, who were both born in Guinea. Our prayer is that our lives be a flower of sweet perfume to the Lord and to fellow human beings.' Barka is one of the princes of pioneering in Africa.

The Chadian contribution echoes what happened in Antioch in Acts 11. The church in Antioch began after Christians were scattered because of persecution in Jerusalem. Often Christians won't move unless a crisis occurs in their lives. The Chadian dispersion demonstrates how God can turn crises to good, for the blessing of many people.

Let's look at India, the second largest country in the world, rich in diversity with a population of 1.3 billion, speaking 325 languages and 1,625 dialects. I have already mentioned the very significant contribution that the Union of Evangelical Students of India (UESI) has made to world mission. The UESI was formed in the 1950s and now has about 15,000 student and graduate members spread out in 1,200 groups. Between 2000 and 2005, the number of student cells increased by 60%. In 2006 the movement embarked on a gospel distribution programme. There are 150 million students in India's universities. Through these gospels the UESI will reach students in each language group.

From the 1950s, a steady stream started to become engaged in cross-cultural mission, in the Muslim and Hindu heartland in the north, and further afield in the Gulf States, Nepal and Fiji.

P. A. Thomas is one such. In 1980 he was sent by UESI as a young graduate to pioneer the student work in Nepal. He served there for twenty years, building a network of student groups before handing on to K. P. Devkota, the first Nepali General Secretary under whose leadership we are seeing thriving growth with some 2,500 students actively committed to Christ on their campuses. P. A. Thomas still serves in Nepal, training church leaders across the country.

Church growth in Nepal is one of the most remarkable stories of the twentieth century. The country was closed to all Western influence until 1951, when the King returned from exile to form the new government. Although mission agencies were allowed to serve in medical and educational work, a law was passed forbidding citizens from changing their religion. This law, which lasted thirty-five years, imposed a penalty of three years in prison which was meted out to hundreds of Nepali Christians over that time. During the 1970s and 1980s, most Nepali evangelists and many pastors were jailed. The first church opened in 1954 and by 1970 there were about 1,000 evangelicals in the country. After a huge surge in growth since the turn of the century, there are today well over 300,000 (some estimating more than double that number). I have been impressed by young Nepali graduates who have formed evangelistic teams to neighbouring Bhutan, one of the least-evangelized nations in the world. There is a significant Nepali-speaking minority in Bhutan and Nepalis view it as their 'Samaria'. They can have a much greater impact than Western missionaries.

As the monarchy and government in Nepal are both vulnerable and tension rises quickly, the movement has shown creative and energetic missionary vision, often at personal cost. As I write I think of Kul Prasad, staff worker in the west of the country who was held by the Maoist guerrillas for four or five days in 2005. He was converted from a privileged Brahmin background, attracted by forgiveness which alone is found in Christ – he received a lot of opposition from his family. Today he walks or cycles between student groups because the roads are not good.

Sometimes it takes him three or four days to move from one group to another. Here as elsewhere, the modelling of staff and the training of students go hand-in-hand. In 2006, Upendra, staff worker in the east of the country, gathered a group of students to cycle with him several hundred kilometres along the southern border, and share the gospel with students on campuses as they went. How beautiful are the feet of those who bring good news.

For many years students and staff from the Korean student movement have had a desire to establish movements in Mongolia, and in the Central Asian Republics of Kazakhstan, Uzbekistan, Azerbaijan, as well as Turkey – all these countries have similar linguistic roots. Despite having a long-time concern for Mongolia, it was impossible to do anything there until the fall of the communist system after 1989. It took some years before the first Korean staff could travel to Mongolia, but in 1997 the Park family arrived in Ulaanbaatar.

Several of the early Christian students had their Bibles confiscated and burned.

After two years of language study they set up cultural exchange camps between Mongolian students and students from Korea, Japan, Hong Kong and the USA. Through these, students from IFES movements in these countries were able to share their faith. Being a Christian is no soft option in this country. For many Mongolians, to be Mongolian is to be Tibetan Buddhist. The small student group that gathered round the Parks was particularly encouraged when the complete Bible was published for the first time in 2000. Some read it right through in the first few months. However, their families did not share their enthusiasm. Several of the early Christian students had their Bibles confiscated and burned along with the careful notes they had taken at dozens of meetings. Nevertheless after many years of prayer, God has begun to build his church among students in that land and we have rejoiced to see the appointment of six Mongolian volunteer staff.

One young couple used greatly in strengthening the Mongolian movement are Tom and Nancy Lin. Tom writes:

> Fewer than two and a half million people live in this vast country with thirty three million sheep, horses, cows, camels and goats! Mongolia has a nomadic culture, one of the coldest winters in the world and poverty-stricken people. About 95% of Mongolians practise some sort of Tibetan Buddhism, and in 1989 there were almost no known Christians. Pioneering a student movement here has its challenges. The Park family who came from IVF-Korea began studying the gospel with a small group of non-believers in the capital, Ulaanbaatar. Four years later around sixty students were taking part in meetings; half of them not yet Christians.

Tom and Nancy Lin's story

Tom, who comes from a Christian family of Chinese immigrants from Taiwan, studied economics at Harvard. After his graduation, he met and married Nancy and the two stayed at Harvard, joining the staff of Intervarsity/USA.

They both wanted to explore opportunities to serve overseas, and when they were in their mid-twenties an opportunity arose. Opposition from Tom's family meant they faced a stark choice: go to Mongolia in obedience to God's call, without the blessing of Tom's parents, or find a job in Chicago near his family, as they wanted him to do. They obeyed God's call and moved to the capital city of Ulaanbaatar where God has powerfully used them – with others – to build up student work. There are now three large groups in that city.

Despite these encouragements, an ongoing sadness was the family rift caused by Tom and Nancy's move. After several years away, Tom decided to attempt reconciliation and turned up one Christmas at his parents' home. They allowed him in but did not speak to him for the whole Christmas season. It was a difficult period for them all.

Not long afterwards Tom learnt that his mother had cancer and wanted to see him. When he arrived she acknowledged that she had done wrong and asked forgiveness for cutting him off. Longing to be reconciled to him, she urged him to keep serving Christ. Their reconciliation was very precious – she died a month later. After Tom's mother died, Tom's father also asked forgiveness and the two were reconciled. His father has now encouraged him to continue serving the Lord wherever he senses God is calling him. The Lins have now returned to the USA where Tom serves as a Regional Director for Intervarsity.

Stories from Kenya

The triennial Kenya missions conferences (called 'Commission') were based on the Urbana model, and have been a wonderful stimulus for Africa-based mission. It was at 'Commission 88' that a student called Francis Omondi committed himself to serve God cross-culturally. Francis is the founding director of Sheepfold Ministries. 'I longed to see a Kenyan agency which would serve among the unreached,' he said. Now Sheepfold Ministries has over seventy cross-cultural workers and is planting churches in Kenya, Tanzania, Ethiopia and Somalia.

Three years later at 'Commission 91' God met in a special way with Eric Simiyu, a final-year student at Kenyatta University. After hearing about the plight of 370,000 refugees arriving in Kenya from Sudan, Somalia and Ethiopia, he rallied students to visit a refugee camp in Kakuma in the north-west of the country. Seeing people in makeshift homes, with malnourished and sometimes sexually abused children, shocked them. The students helped with literacy classes, trained the refugees in how to generate income, and preached in the camp churches. They led many to Christ. When they returned to university the group met weekly to pray for refugees and to learn more about Muslim evangelism. Eric and several others learned the Amharic language.

Every year FOCUS Kenya runs a mission to an unreached people group. I recall hearing of how two truckloads of students went to the Samburu and Turkana people, about 400 km from Nairobi, where many had no school education and few had heard about Christ. The students brought encouragement and extra help to the Christian Samburu students and local pastors. The first four days were spent in training, prayer and fasting, and in studying Jesus' example in public ministry. They then spent each morning going from house to house, talking of their faith in Christ, and each afternoon preaching and doing drama in the open air. They were amazed at the effect of the gospel as it was preached for the first time in some places. A few of the hearers resisted to the point of manhandling the students, chasing them away with insults and threats. But the majority listened, asked questions, and discussed – many committed their lives to Christ.

One group led by a medical student spent three days in a village, where they were warmly welcomed. The combination they brought of medical care and gospel proclamation led to a rich response. Another student organized a meeting for the local tough Samburu warriors and fifteen came. When the gospel was explained, several bowed in humility to trust Christ. In eight days over 1,000 people professed faith! So students boldly exercised their talents in evangelism while learning to pray and take responsibility for mission themselves.

Integral mission

In some circles in the West, evangelicals have withdrawn from social responsibility, fearing that over-emphasis on practical needs could diminish a focus on proclaiming the gospel. The 1974 Lausanne Congress addressed the matter and showed clearly the biblical teaching for what we now call 'integral mission'.[7] There is good historical precedent for holding the two in creative tension. Vishal Mangalwadi in his book *William Carey and the Regeneration of India* shows the breadth of Carey's ministry. He not only moved from village to village sharing the message of Jesus with people he met, and translated the Bible into many languages, but he also:

- lectured on science, drawing on his botany
- introduced the steam engine and encouraged blacksmiths to make copies
- brought in the idea of savings banks to prevent people from unscrupulous money lenders
- campaigned for humane treatment of leprosy patients
- introduced printing technology
- established the first newspaper in any oriental language
- stood against the oppression of women and ministered to the poor

Students in Latin America

Let me give two examples of how students have tried to apply this within their own cultures in Latin America.

Charo Ameztegui, wife of the then General Secretary of the Bolivian movement, founded a ministry called *Mosoj Yan* (a Quechua phrase meaning 'New Way') to support young street girls in Cochabamba. The aim is to help these girls transform their lives and their situations and to find fullness of life through meeting with the living Christ. Her initiative grew out of the conviction she formed as a student – that our mission is one of evangelism and serving.

Bolivia is a country of contrasts: a rich land, full of beautiful and diverse landscapes and geography. At the same time, it is the poorest country in Latin America with high rates of infant mortality, illiteracy and unemployment. Many families work hard to survive and 'a child who does not work, does not eat'. This reality is harder still for girls who in a machismo culture must leave school to take on responsibilities from an early age – those who cannot bear the pressure and violence in their homes escape to live on the streets.

Many CCU students have been involved in *Mosoj Yan* as volunteers, and graduates have served on staff or as Board members. What began as a small aid project has turned into a programme of care with a diversified work in prevention, motivation and rehabilitation. Charo writes, 'We have witnessed miracles in the lives of the girls, as we walk with them through their human misery and pain. We have experienced frustrations and we have wept. But we have learned that however great the need, God's power and provision are greater still.'

In Colombia students took to the streets in October 1999 with millions of other Colombians, shouting '*No mas*' (no more violence). A plane on which Grace Morillo, UCU Colombia staff, was travelling had been hijacked earlier that year – she was held hostage for two months. (Grace's story is in Chapter 8.)

We must take a stand against the language of guns, landmines, terrorism.

'I have on my desk a map of Colombia,' wrote the General Secretary, Alvin Gongora. 'It shows in red the regions where violence is being carried out by guerrillas, right-wing death squads and the army. Shame on us, the whole map is red: 798 militia parties out of 1,102! As a nation, we are waking up to say weapons have no right to shape our future. We in the student movement confess a God whose name is the Prince of Peace, so we must take a stand against the language of guns, landmines, terrorism, marching boots and the drafting of kids into military tanks.'

'At the end of the march in Simon Bolivar Park in Bogotá, as we joined in the singing with two million voices, we made a circle to pray, bringing to God the sin of our nation, and asking him to bless us with his forgiving presence. May the Lord mobilize his Church in Colombia for his glory and the good of the nation.'

The movement, approaching its fortieth anniversary, has groups in twelve cities, with a core of some 150 students out of the nation's one million students. Grace Morillo, who now serves as General Secretary, writes:

> Colombia is facing a social and economic crisis, and is caught up in multiple conflicts. The evangelical Church continues to grow and there is a great thirst for meaning and hope.
>
> Historically universities were associated with leftist sympathies but now they tend towards the extreme right. We have heard of several university professors being shot dead. Some public universities are in the control of armed groups.
>
> There is pressure on universities to reduce their budget and compete within the global market, so fees are being raised, programs reduced, and there are fewer scholarships for students from provincial cities. We are saddened by this move as we love the university and we do not believe it will enhance its development.
>
> We do not want our students to be strangers to the social and political situation in which they live. We encourage them to be involved in integral mission and to understand the life-giving influence which the gospel can have on all aspects of society and life. Our graduates serve as pastors, in the caring professions, in the government and in private enterprise.

The aspiration of the movement is expressed in its motto: 'Jesus Christ in the University, consolation and justice for all humanity.'

Partnership in mission

I have already mentioned our partnership with mission agencies. This value of partnership is rooted in passages such as Philippians 1:4–11.

In all my prayers for all of you, I always pray with joy because of your partnership in the gospel from the first day until now, being confident of this, that he who began a good work in you will carry it on to completion until the day of Christ Jesus.

It is right for me to feel this way about all of you, since I have you in my heart; for whether I am in chains or defending and confirming the gospel, all of you share in God's grace with me. God can testify how I long for all of you with the affection of Christ Jesus.

And this is my prayer: that your love may abound more and more in knowledge and depth of insight, so that you may be able to discern what is best and may be pure and blameless until the day of Christ, filled with the fruit of righteousness that comes through Jesus Christ – to the glory and praise of God.

Here we see partnership in the early church based on common beliefs and a common commitment to the gospel (v. 5); a common trust in the good purposes of God (v. 6); a common experience of God's grace (v. 7); and a common love rooted in Christ (v. 8) and covered in prayer (v. 9).

IFES and mission agencies serve the church in ways which are hard to separate. That partnership can be seen at different levels. At the level of mission strategists, of board members and of workers in the harvest field, we have strong ties. Almost all the IFES movements in East Asia were founded by OMF missionaries. Interserve, SAMS, Latin Link, LAM, Arab World Ministries and CMS Australia have all contributed significantly by seconding experienced staff to work in the university context.

Operation Mobilisation, SIM, WEC and Wycliffe Bible translators are never far from student groups, giving robust training to students in their vacations or after they graduate, and opening their worlds to new horizons. I myself spent a year on the OM ship *Logos* and owe a great debt of gratitude to God for that formative experience.

In turn, IFES movements nurture the faith of missionaries in their student years, and help them see that mission is part of the character of God. World mission is one of the three aims of every campus group and IFES publishing houses take seriously the need to produce mission biographies and other books on mission for students and graduates. Many staff and graduates of IFES movements have gone on to serve with mission agencies – it is a well-trodden path.

It has become fashionable to refer to IFES and to mission agencies as 'para-church movements'. My preference is instead to use the term 'intra-church movement', for we are part of the church, and exist only in relation to it. We *serve* the church. There are different roles and functions for different parts of the body, and members have different gifts. Student ministry is essentially a specialist ministry of the church, obeying Christ's call to reach into the part of the world that happens to be the university, so it is an arm of the church into the student world, a link between the local church and the student community.

Many staff and graduates have gone on to serve with mission agencies.

At the start of this book we looked at the place of the university in the nation, and its long and inescapable arm into every aspect of society. In human terms, what happens in the university will determine the freedom of the church. So IFES movements are dedicated to universities and colleges, whereas mission agencies fulfil a different and complementary brief. They are engaged in church planting, literature work, radio ministry, village evangelism, bringing the gospel to a rich and diverse range of peoples. If you support a mission agency, perhaps you would pray for the student ministry in that country or on that continent too? (I have included a guide for prayer on pages 200–204.)

How to develop a world mission mindset

Feed your mind
- Read magazines and webzines from mission agencies and mission biographies
- Go to a missions conference
- Invite mission speakers to your churches or student groups
- Study mission in the Bible – put your mind under the persuasive light of Scripture

Get involved
- Join an evangelistic summer team or year team
- Get to know international students
- Give sacrificially in the spirit of Alexander Duff who said: 'If I can't go, I'll send a substitute.'
- Join or start a prayer group
- Use newspapers, the web, *Operation World* or mission magazines to help you pray
- Send postcards of encouragement to missionaries – it doesn't take long to write a postcard!

5 : Making a difference in society

One of the best tests of student ministry is the impact its graduates
are making ten and twenty years later.
(Dr Bobby Sng, former General Secretary of FES Singapore and
Vice-Chairman of the IFES Executive Committee)

To try to improve society is not worldliness but love. To wash your
hands of society is not love but worldliness.
(Sir Fred Catherwood, former IFES Vice-President and a former
Vice-President of the European Union)

In our opening chapter we looked at Daniel. Let's turn our minds
back to him now.

Daniel was surrounded by hostile opponents who would do
anything to discredit him; he was faced with morally comprom-
ising situations and had trouble with his supervisors. He is a
wonderful example to us; he served three kings, exercising
influence in a court full of intrigue and infected by idolatry for over
sixty years.

We read in Daniel 6:3–5:

Now Daniel so distinguished himself among the administrators and the satraps by his exceptional qualities that the king planned to set him over the whole kingdom. At this, the administrators and the satraps tried to find grounds for charges against Daniel in his conduct of government affairs, but they were unable to do so. They could find no corruption in him, because he was trustworthy and neither corrupt nor negligent. Finally these men said, 'We will never find any basis for charges against this man Daniel unless it has something to do with the law of his God.'

What a powerful testimony! We have other examples in the lives of Joseph and Nehemiah. It is a mystery to me how some Christians feel service in the secular world is somehow inferior to more overt forms of Christian ministry. We are called to be salt in our society, saving it from moral decay. I am reminded of the salutary warning that all it takes for evil to triumph is for good men to do nothing.[1] In IFES we are committed to raising up Daniels, Josephs, Nehemiahs and Deborahs.

We are committed to raising up Daniels, Josephs, Nehemiahs and Deborahs.

Following in their steps, graduates of our student movements in some of the toughest contexts are taking very bold stands against moral corruption. I think of the Democratic Republic of Congo, a country which has suffered through civil war and brutality in ways we can barely imagine. The IFES movement there was founded in the mid 1990s and three staff serve some 2,500 students. The volcanic eruption in Goma in 2002 brought terrible devastation. Not long beforehand, at an evangelistic camp, many students had professed faith in Christ. Now families were stripped of all their material and financial means and the Goma GBU office and library were destroyed. Out of their own poverty, students in Kinshasa

How one businessman invested for the gospel

A secular career can open unusual doors for gospel ministry. The student movements right across Africa trace their beginnings to an Oxford graduate who first entered the colonial service, then served in business. He was never in paid Christian ministry but his legacy for the gospel has been immense.

Tony Wilmot was one of the outstanding graduates of his generation.[2] As Senior Cypher Officer in the East Africa Campaign he rose to the rank of lieutenant-colonel and was mentioned in dispatches. He became Secretary to the Government in British Somaliland, then, as Permanent Secretary to the Ministry of Communication and Works, saw through such projects as the construction of the Volta Dam and Tema Harbour.

Despite these demanding jobs and a growing family, he accepted the invitation of the British Inter-Varsity Fellowship (now UCCF), to gauge the possibility of pioneering a sister movement in Africa. As Tony travelled on business, he sought out Christian students with leadership gifts. Drawing on his own student experience he helped them to set up Bible study groups and to see the need to be firmly grounded in the faith. Gradually the Pan African Fellowship of Evangelical Students was formed, and from there the national movements across the continent grew. The Nigerian Fellowship of Evangelical Students (NIFES) is currently the largest movement in the world with some 40,000 students.

Tony had an unusual gift of sensing who would rise to positions of influence, and investing in them. He and his wife, Eve, held weekly Bible classes in their home and regular members included: Yakubu Gowan, later military governor of Nigeria; Jerry Gana, later Nigeria's Minister for Information (see p. 118); Emeka Anyaoku, later Secretary General of the Commonwealth; and Philemon Quaye, later Commodore of the Ghanaian navy and then Ghana's ambassador to Liberia and Egypt.

Tony was committed to strengthening the African Church. While student ministry played a major role, another strategic initiative was needed. African Christian leaders needed theological training beyond first degree level, within the African context. At the age of sixty-four this modern-day Caleb embarked on a new major project, working to found a theological college for postgraduate study. He and Eve travelled throughout Europe, America and Australia to raise the required funding and in 1979 purchased eighteen acres outside Nairobi, then housing three chicken runs and a dog food factory! That scene illustrated a profound characteristic of the man. He looked at what was and saw what could be. In 1983 the Nairobi Evangelical Graduate School of Theology (NEGST) was opened with a Zimbabwean dean, four students and Tony as principal. Within its first twenty years it had trained 200 pastors and theological teachers. That number is now growing significantly.

rallied to send 100 kg of clothes to their brothers and sisters in Goma. They then did the same for students in Mbandaka in the north of the country. Here family members were sharing clothes with each other, taking it in turns to go out, as there were not enough for everyone. 'Just like the Macedonians, we did what we were able to according to our small means,' wrote Hubert Miyimi, then General Secretary. They were indeed like the Macedonians, giving in fact *beyond* their means.

They were indeed like the Macedonians, giving beyond their means.

Graduates of the GBU lend help to the students where they can, and some of these graduates have been appointed to positions of high influence. A national church movement has been started to nurture 'Daniels and Josephs of our time' to meet the economic and political challenges. The president of the church movement is a graduate of GBU.

Corruption in the universities has reached new depths. Men

students must pay bribes to pass their exams. For the women the cost is higher. Some are required to have sexual relations with their lecturers to receive pass grades, the top grades reserved for those who do not use protection. At the University of Kinshasa, staff are dying of AIDS, and many are HIV positive. It is a cruel requirement and wreaking further agonies for families in years to come as people struggle with the disease, and leave orphaned children behind them. While urging Christian women not to give in, the GBU has rallied help from television channels and local radio to bring pressure on the government to put a stop to it.

Yet even in this hour of great need, the students are looking beyond their own borders and planning regular world missions conventions.

The trilemma

The church has always struggled with its approach to the world, taking one of three positions:

Separation
Here Christians cut themselves off from the world, believing the only worthwhile activity is to evangelize or attend church meetings. This is what John Stott calls 'rabbit hole Christianity'. Rabbits put their heads out of their burrows and then, if there is no-one about, race onto open land to find food and swiftly return to their burrows. Christians can be like that, dashing to Christian activities, with minimal contact with the world. This breeds a hit-and-run form of evangelism, not to be despised but not the best way to reach out to people. It assumes the world is intrinsically evil.

Accommodation
Here Christians urge that we should simply join in, to the extent of becoming like the world. This can lead to an indistinguishable lifestyle. These people tend to speak little and rarely about the

glory of Christ. You could describe them as baptizing the latest secular notions with Christian meaning, rather than challenging the non-Christian world-view with biblical principles and biblical teaching. This perspective usually arises from liberal theology.

Engagement

Here Christians seek to engage with society. In Jeremiah 29:5–7 the exiles in Babylon are urged to 'build houses and settle down; plant gardens and eat what they produce. Marry and have sons and daughters ... seek peace and prosperity'. Christians are to be morally distinct but not socially segregated from the world – to be in but not of the world. This seems to be echoed in Jesus' high-priestly prayer in John 17: 'I pray not that you will take them out of the world. As you sent me, so I send them.' It is difficult to engage with the world while retaining our saltiness, but that is what we are called to do.

There are many examples of such engagement from the history of IFES. Let us start in Bolivia. Ana was a university student and a volunteer staff worker at the same time. One of her professors would not give her a pass grade in her subject until she had sexual relations with him. Ana refused to sleep with the professor and he refused to award her a pass grade for several years running. Eventually he gave her the pass grade, realizing he was not going to wear her down. After passing the exam she got a job in a clinic which turned out to be full of corruption and carried out illegal abortions. Courageously she wrote a letter of resignation, explaining all her reasons for leaving. The owner of the clinic telephoned her a few days later: 'I do not accept your resignation. Would you please stay?' The owner went on to explain that he wanted her to become director of the clinic. He had been so impressed by the reports he had heard of her, and of the way she was weathering the criticism and disdain of her senior colleagues, that it caused him to ask questions and to reappraise his own situation. Did he really want to make money from a clinic that had such little regard for its patients?

Isn't that wonderful! As a student she had learned to love the
Lord and had been faithful under pressure. On graduation she
transformed a clinic of very poor quality and bad reputation into
an exemplary one and news of it spread through the city. The
power of the gospel can change one student's life, then a clinic. It
can influence a city – and why not a country?

When Fanny Bejarano was converted to Christ as a student in
Argentina, she began to learn and to practise a lifestyle of holiness,
mercy, compassion, respect and dignity. This led to problems
professionally, so much so that she had to forego promotion. At
twenty-one she joined the judiciary, full of energy and impetuos-
ity, wanting to be a judge. After working in a court of first instance,
then a Criminal Court, she finally reached the superior Court of
Justice in her province. At the Attorney General's office she met
judges who were corrupt, deceitful and mendacious. Day by day
she sought to live in a counter-cultural fashion. Her boss had
several adulterous relationships and ordered her to tell lies for him.
She refused, so she was unpopular. However, she was able to tell
her colleagues about the gospel of Christ and give them New
Testaments.

Her supervisor, however, remained indifferent to her. After
having been denied promotion on three occasions, she spoke with
the judge in the Senior Judiciary, who placed her in a position of
prominence where she is able to serve Christ freely and openly.
Fanny was committed to having a salty influence in her country.

We must help graduates to view the world as a place God has
created, and to be courageous – even in the toughest and most
corrupt societies.

A biblical view of work

Daniel had a positive view of the world, and also of work. The
difficulty of relating our faith to our work is not new. The Greek
philosopher Aristotle argued that to be unemployed was good

fortune because it allowed a person to participate in political life and contemplation. Greek society was organized so that a few could enjoy the blessing of leisure whilst slaves did the work. This view of work was later propagated by the Medieval Church. Thus the priestly or monastic vocation was considered far superior to ordinary, everyday work. It was from Martin Luther that the sixteenth-century Reformers recovered a sense that our work could be understood as a calling from God. The Dutch theologian and politician Abraham Kuyper put it so memorably when he said, 'There is not one centimetre of human existence to which Christ, who is Lord of all, does not point and say: "That is mine!" '

The story of work begins in Genesis 1 where we meet God at work creating the cosmos. Its significance and dignity for us stems from our being made in the image of a working God. Genesis 2 portrays people acting as co-workers with God in creating families, gathering food, cultivating the earth, naming the animals and being given responsibility for the care and stewardship of creation. From the beginning, God's creativity and human work are intimately connected. In Genesis 3 we are confronted with the destructive impact

God's creativity and human work are intimately connected.

of sin on the world, on work, and with the pain and struggle that ensued. Now to God's creative and sustaining work is added his redeeming work. From here onwards the Bible is full of examples of partnership between God and us in this work of redemption.

To understand this, it is worth reflecting on what we know of the work of Bible characters: many produce goods (cattle farmers, vineyard tenders, iron workers, carpenters, tent makers); some are managers (of grain supplies, of employees, of building projects, in armies) or financiers; some are public servants (in medicine, courts, community, public finance); some are artists (musicians, sculptors, dancers, writers). By including them in the sacred record, we know that God does not view these people and their efforts as ignoble.

Our own worth lies in our being created in God's image, and being co-creators with him.

God the Creator and daily worker is vitally involved in restoring his handiwork. Let us not slip back into the deist view of him as a watchmaker who winds up what he has made and leaves the scene. Scripture portrays a Creator who actively holds all things together (Colossians 1:17; Hebrews 1:3). As those created in his image, we should work with him. Note that when Jesus found himself in a controversy over the Sabbath, he asserted 'My father is always at work to this very day, and I, too, am working' (John 5:17).

A wrong view of work can lead to a wrong view of heaven. We sometimes hear eternal life described as some kind of eternal choir, but Isaiah and the apostle John speak of work in heaven, work that is painless, effective and fulfilling. In Isaiah 65 we read of home building and harvesting without sweat or toil in the new heavens and new earth. In Revelation 22 John portrays the monthly harvests. We will work in heaven without sweat and toil, but we will certainly work! God's original design for work comes in Genesis 1 and before the fall – that design will be restored in heaven.

A wrong view of work can lead to a wrong view of heaven.

Monday through to Friday is not just a long dark tunnel between weekends. If so, the Sabbath becomes a weak parenthesis between drudgery. No, the working week is central to our nature as co-creators with God, and the Sabbath is the point where we join him in rest and celebration of all that we have done together. It is a time to reflect on our work and, in the words of Genesis, to reflect on the fact that 'it is good'. When we make no effort to recover work as one of the primary ways in which we reflect God's image, we become worldly and we participate in the

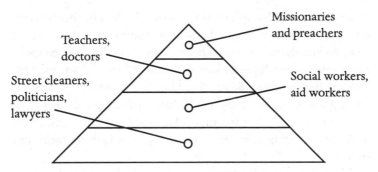

Figure 2. Some Christians wrongly perceive the scale of spiritual significance like this.

worldly myth that work is a necessary evil. We deny the very nature of God as creator/worker and we demean humanity.

Our jobs put us in touch with people like no other activity except family life. For forty plus hours a week we toil, laugh, struggle and care together. To view a job only as a platform for evangelism is utilitarian and unfair to employers. Paul addressed this by calling early believers to obedience to employers, fairness towards employees, hard work and avoidance of idleness. In each of these Paul reflects a high view of both the worker and the work.

The world is waiting for a new breed of Christians who hold a high view of work and of God's blessing on it.

Some roles give opportunity for expressing God's compassion. As a result of the killings by the *Sendero Luminoso* in Peru in the 1990s, many children of Christian workers had been traumatized, having seen their parents shot before their very eyes. They were brought to the capital city, Lima, where they were cared for by Christians and counselled by three young Christian psychologists. Working through the country's Evangelical Alliance, these graduates had decided to use their training to help the children adjust to the loss of their parents.

They introduced them into families in the capital city where they were cared for and adopted. They told me that often the children were unable to say much about the loss of their parents for a year or more because they were so traumatized, but, as time wore on and the women won their confidence, the children spoke more freely – gradually emotional healing began. Two of these women had received death threats from *Sendero Luminoso* for helping the orphans. They could have earned good salaries as professional counsellors in other ways in society, but chose to use their gifts in sacrificial service, integrating their faith and academic studies.

But we must not fall into the error of thinking that the caring professions are superior to the world of commerce. I think of a young graduate of the Russian student movement, an entrepreneur who through hard work and sacrifice had been able to open a small shop in his community. Such endeavours are a vital part of rebuilding shattered economies and this young man believed God had gifted him for such a role and he was doing his best to honour him in his work. It is not easy to retain Christian values in the hugely competitive environment of small businesses at that stage of economic recovery. In church, however, people did not see him as needing prayer in his daily life. Rather he constantly faced questions about why he was not becoming a pastor or missionary. Struggling with these questions, he came to an IFES graduates' conference. Through the Bible expositions he learned that most Bible heroes were just like him, including businessmen and women (e.g. Priscilla and Aquila in Acts 18). For the first time he felt affirmed and free to serve God through his business. He understood that he was not a second-class Christian – he was a worker like God was a worker.

There is dignity in all work and our calling is to please Christ and not just our boss in whatever we do, for, as Paul exhorts the Colossians, 'It is the Lord Christ you are serving' (Colossians 3:24). To take the aroma of Christ onto the factory floor, into the classroom, or into the financial markets is tough. There will always be a need for Christians to bring a salty influence to their professions.

Evangelists, pastors, teachers

One expression of having a Christian mind is to discern whether God may be calling us into a more overt form of Christian ministry, perhaps while we are still students, or later when we are in a profession. If he does, we will find ourselves facing a range of questions about prestige, success, financial security. But, as Thomas Aquinas wrote, 'God is no man's debtor'.[3]

In every generation there is an urgent need for gifted evangelists, pastors and teachers who will play a special role in preparing God's people for works of service, 'so that the body of Christ may be built up until we all reach unity in the faith and in the knowledge of the Son of God and become mature, attaining to the whole measure of the fulness of Christ' (Ephesians 4:12–14). This is the true perspective in which to view that calling – as servants of Christ who are working with him to bring his church into maturity.

It is a high calling and it can be costly.

IFES movements have nurtured the early spiritual lives of countless evangelists, pastors and teachers for the church at home and across cultures: graduates, often with remarkable gifting, who have pressed their skills into gospel ministry. It is a high calling and it can be costly. But those who have spent their lives in spiritual ministry count it as a privilege and joy. You read in the last chapter of our strong commitment to world mission and how thousands of IFES graduates are serving the church.

It has long been the prayer of IFES movements that every university town and city would have at least one church with a strong preaching and teaching ministry. We are seeing a wonderful pattern emerge of such churches around the world, often led by IFES graduates. May God continue to call students from every generation to serve in this vital way.[4]

Courage and honour

Now I want to take you to Guinea-Bissau in West Africa. The government often sent its brightest students to study in Portugal, with which it has strong links. In the 1980s Procel DaSilva Armando studied law there. During that time he became a Christian and began to grow in his faith. Through friends in the Christian Union, he learned how the Bible applies to every area of life and resolved on returning home to work to influence his country's government and legal services. He was very able and was quickly appointed as Deputy to the Chief Justice. Guinea-Bissau, a one-party state, had a small church. Some counsellors around the President spoke to him rather as the counsellors did to Nebuchadnezzar in the time of Daniel, recommending that freedom of worship be restricted because of the growing influence of Christians. The President listened, and asked the Chief Justice to draw up a new law which would restrict such freedom. The Chief Justice in turn delegated the responsibility to Procel.

Procel agonized over this, but realized he had no choice in how to respond. So taking his life in his hands, he respectfully told the President that he had to decline. 'Why do you refuse?' the President asked. The young man replied, 'I am a Christian. I could not frame a law restricting the activities of my brothers and sisters in Christ. You must do with me as you will.' The President was so impressed with Procel's firm but gracious stance that he abandoned the new law! Even in corrupt regimes, integrity is appreciated by many in leadership. Ten years later the President invited Procel to become Prime Minister of the country. He turned down the invitation because he didn't want to be too closely associated with the President. So the President offered him any position in the cabinet he would care to choose. He took the position of Head of Communications so that he would have control over television and newspapers. In due course, Procel was to become the key person to arrange for the formal registration of the young student ministry.

Tragically, he and his family were involved in a car crash. His wife and child were killed, but he was spared and flown in the presidential jet to Paris so he could receive excellent medical attention. After a long convalescence he returned to Guinea-Bissau, where he is now First Secretary of the Parliament.

In his story we can see both faith and deliverance in the midst of adversity. One humble believer who landed in Portugal as an overseas student was able to become a Daniel at court back in his home country. We should never underestimate the influence that someone with courage can bring on the whole direction of a culture. C. S. Lewis says the central lessons from the book of Daniel are the importance of Christian friendship and the impact Christians can make on another culture. That impact can be far-reaching. Robert Bellah, the US sociologist, reckons it takes only 2% of a population who share an active common vision for a just and a gentle society to effect change.

'I have been like Daniel'

We can see both faith and deliverance in the midst of adversity.

Rwanda was profoundly shaken by internecine warfare between Hutus and Tutsis in 1994. Perhaps as many as 800,000 people were killed in this fighting over the 100-day period, and as many as a million died in total, including those infected by disease or by AIDS as a result of rape. During that time Charles Muligande, a graduate who had been active in the student ministry, was teaching in a university in the USA. After the fighting subsided, he was invited back to the country to serve as Minister of Transport in the government.

Because of his commitment to being a salty influence in his own culture, he gave up a good salary in the USA to return to what was still a very unstable country. He became Principal of the National University of Rwanda in Butare, and then Foreign Secretary.

When I visited the country, he was the university principal. He arranged a banquet at which I was asked to speak to the university professors. I spoke about the model of Daniel who feared God and sought to be an influence in Babylonian society, which was a culture deeply given to corruption and superstition – and yet Daniel retained his distinctive witness to the God of the Bible amid all the dramatic changes in that nation, serving three kings over forty years.

After I finished speaking, Charles Muligande got up and said, 'You know that I've been like a Daniel before you. I have not given into corrupt practices. I've governed the university fairly, and sought to apply biblical values and justice in all my dealings. So as Daniel commended the God of the Old Testament to the Babylonians, I commend the God of the Bible to you.' There was a stunned silence. Everyone knew that what Charles said was true. His Christian testimony was exemplary. May God use IFES to raise up more like Charles Muligande.

The HIV/AIDS pandemic

As anyone who knows the student culture is aware, sexual promiscuity is widespread, and the HIV virus has travelled fast through the student world, especially in the Caribbean where the virus is spreading most quickly, and in Sub-Saharan Africa, where its incidence in the general population is highest. For up-to-date figures see the UN AIDS website at www.unaids.org.

IFES is working with other Christian agencies, local government and educational initiatives, and with the World Health Organization to serve students as best we are able – those students who are infected and those who are not.

In South Africa the IFES movement produced Bible studies from Luke's Gospel under the title *Ses'khona*, a Zulu word meaning 'we are here'. It helps Christian students see the Lord's compassion for the suffering. We are here to walk with you in your pain – we are here to love you and serve you. The cover shows four students carrying the coffin of a friend on their shoulders. In front is a fifth student, resolutely leading the way holding a cross.

The IFES movement in Malawi has won wide respect for its abstinence campaign, urging high school pupils and students, whether they are Christians or not, to abstain from sexual relations outside marriage. Its leaflets *Abstinence: is it a practical option?* and *Safe sex? You must be joking!* have had huge printruns, and give a Christian apologetic for sexual purity. The movement has trained 300 students to encourage others in their local groups and to present the argument for purity.

Staff in all our affected movements have worked on action plans following regional consultations. We need prayer as staff help Christian students to apply Scripture to their lifestyles and as we work more broadly to help influence the way students think.

What is important about such people, of course, is that they develop what we might call 'a Christian mind', that is, a Christian world-view. That term was first coined by Professor Daniel Lamont in one of the early conferences of what was to become the IFES movement, in the 1930s. It has been popularized since by the writings of Harry Blamires and of John Stott.[5] To develop a Christian mind fulfils three criteria. *First*, it glorifies our Creator who has made us as rational creatures in his own image and wants us to explore his revelation in nature and Scripture. *Second*, it enriches our Christian life as we can worship God only when we know who he is and reflect on his glory. Faith rests on a knowledge of God's character. *Third*, it strengthens our evangelistic witness. Many times in the book of Acts we read of the apostles reasoning with people and seeking to persuade them. As we saw earlier, faith and reason are not contrasted in Scripture – it is faith and sight that are held in contrast. Jesus challenged Thomas to believe 'having not seen', not 'having not thought'.

The Holy Spirit brings people to faith in Jesus when he opens their minds to examine the evidence. It is useless to have Christians in positions of authority if they do not have a Christian mind. In the 1980s Rios Del Montt was elected as the first evangelical president in Guatemala in Central America. At that time I met with the IFES staff member working there. I spoke about how wonderful it was to have a Christian president, assuming he would be encouraged by Rios Del Montt's appointment. His response surprised me. 'Lindsay', he said, 'it is a tragedy he has been appointed, for he does not have a Christian mind. Corruption continues; and he appoints relatives to positions of influence and power. So his election as president has actually turned out to be a scandal for the gospel!' These were sobering words.

The importance of legacy

Let me take you to a field west of Abuja, the administrative capital of Nigeria, and to a missions conference for 6,000 students, hosted by the Nigerian Fellowship of Evangelical Students (NIFES) – probably the largest evangelical student conference ever held in Africa. One speaker was Professor Jerry Gana, Nigerian Minister for Information. Prof. Gana had become a Christian through Scripture Union and grew in this faith through NIFES before going to study in Aberdeen, Scotland, where he became the first African president of a British Christian Union. Since returning to Nigeria, he has served for twenty-five years in a position of political influence. He is widely respected by politicians of all backgrounds because of his Christian integrity. I asked him how he had managed to stand firm against corruption all these years.

First, he told me how he had learnt through Scripture Union and NIFES to abide in Christ by observing the lives of the staff workers. Through their example he had sought to walk with the Lord each day, meditating on Scripture and cultivating a disciplined spirit of prayer. He then went on:

'*Second*, in politics you have to choose your friends and partnerships carefully,' he said, 'because if someone develops a bad policy, your reputation could be damaged by association.' He had learned his lesson from how Daniel chose his co-workers. Other Christians had been derailed in Nigerian politics because of their associations with those who proved to be corrupt.

'*Third*, I realize the importance of legacy,' he added. 'I want to help change the political landscape in Nigeria and I believe this can be done through a group of Christians exercising influence, just like the Clapham Sect in London in the early nineteenth century. Think of their influence in the abolition of the slave trade and other ways they introduced biblical values in policies. So I am asking God to give me fifty years, as the political situation in Nigeria cannot be changed overnight.'

Want to be a Daniel?

- Remember that the world is looking for people of integrity.
  The king loved Daniel (Daniel 6:14) because he was a trustworthy adviser. People in senior positions appreciate those whose word is their bond.
- Work out your principles and resolve not to compromise. 'Pity the man who tries to work out his principles in a time of crisis' (Goethe).
- Develop a support group (see Tonica Van der Meer's 'honesty chains' on p. 155).
- Don't rationalize unethical decisions.
- Don't flirt with temptation. Look again at how Joseph responded to Potiphar's wife. He had already resolved that sexual relations with a woman other than his wife would be a wickedness against God, and that the best way to avoid temptation was to run.
- Consider the cost of compromise. A clean conscience is dearly won and can be easily lost. When a conscience is sullied, guilt can be overwhelming.
- Be prepared for sacrifice. If you choose to stand against corruption and hostility, it may be costly.

It sounded rather like a discussion with Daniel who served for sixty years acting as a salty influence in Babylon. Jerry Gana is committed to drawing in younger generations of Christians who will serve in politics and take things further, and investing in them so he can pass on what he has learned. You cannot change the world in three years. We need Christians in public life who are courageously committed to the long haul.

More modern-day Daniels

Daniel remained blameless in a corrupt culture throughout his sixty years of service. They could find no corruption in him. Corruption is endemic in many societies all across the world, and it is a great challenge for Christians to be able to resist such a temptation. Ruly, an Indonesian graduate who studied for a doctorate in Australia and then returned home, was a fine example of a graduate who did this.

He was given authority to decide who would provide electricity to a large part of the country. He put the contract out to tender and received several offers. One large company offered him a personal bribe. He turned it down. They returned with an increased offer – he turned that down too.

They became very angry and asked outright 'Why don't you take a bribe? Everyone else does!' Almost without thinking, and clearly helped by the Holy Spirit he replied, 'I will not take your bribe because I have already been bought by the precious blood of Jesus Christ, and you cannot give me anything worth more than that.' The two men were dumbfounded. Over the next two days they each returned, on their own, to ask forgiveness. In this strongly Muslim culture, one had come from a Protestant background and the other a Roman Catholic background. They were rebuked by the conduct of this real believer.

I heard that story as Ruly shared it with a jammed hall of students in Singapore. Here was a married man with a child, whom God had helped stand firm in the face of a tempting offer. Suddenly the students were leaping up in the air, shouting and cheering. They may have felt defeatist until then, but this man had not been defeated. He had set them an attractive example, and their cheering showed how profoundly challenged they had been by it.

Samuel Olofin was Professor of Economics at Nigeria's prestigious Ibadan University. A graduate of Harvard, he served as Chairman of the NIFES Board and Vice-Chairman of the IFES International Executive Committee. Under the regime of General Abacha corruption was unchecked. Prof. Olofin, a mild-mannered man, wrote an open letter to the president pleading with him to restrain the influences of evil. He knew his life might be under threat as a result.

At that time he came to an IFES conference in North America. Many encouraged him not to return, and perhaps to take a position in a US university, but he was determined to go back to Nigeria. I asked him why. His reply was striking. 'I wish to return because it is my country and I do not believe God has made me Nigerian by mistake!' What a sobering challenge. This brother could speak with authority because he was free of corruption himself and had attained a position of prominence as a university lecturer. It was no small decision to return to Nigeria. The situation grew more and more intolerable for Christians and the leaders of NIFES called the whole movement to concerted prayer for change. General Abacha died suddenly in 1998 and we believe the Lord used the prayers of students and graduates to help bring about this change. After a short spell under his deputy, the country elected its first Christian president, Olusegun Obasanjo.

We need Christians in every area of society to remain free of corruption and to function as beacons of hope to their generation. Thank God for such people.

Let me finish with a story from Mexico. In 2002, public transport in Vera Cruz was privatized. Fare increases seemed inevitable and half fares for students were to disappear. Edwin

Gomez was one of the student representatives elected to meet with the transport leader. At this meeting, the transport official proposed giving students a 25% discount, but they rejected that. A few days later they were invited for a luxurious dinner and offered personal benefits if they stayed quiet. Finally, they were each handed an envelope with 80,000 pesos in cash (US $8,000). After struggling with the temptation to accept, Edwin stood up and said no, and handed his back. He could see the reproachful looks from other students. Then a girl rose to her feet and supported him. Gradually they all gave the envelopes back. The transport staff were amazed at their uprightness and resolved not to increase fares. It was a wonderful work of the Holy Spirit in Edwin's life that evening, helping him resist this bribe. As he left, he put his hands in his pockets – he had only four pesos.

May God raise up an army of Daniels.

In Mexico Christian students do not just speak of being 'salt and light', or of living in a way that denounces destructive forces. They speak of wishing to be 'sparkles of hope' in the university world. I love that expression.

There are many students and graduates around the IFES world who have dared to act like Daniel over the last fifty years. May God raise up an army of Daniels in the next generation.

6 : The reconciling power of the gospel

Here there is no Greek or Jew, circumcised or uncircumcised,
barbarian, Scythian, slave or free, but Christ is all, and is in all.
(Colossians 3:11)

I love Serbs because Jesus loves me and they are my brothers
and sisters in Christ.
(a Croatian student)

In the late 1960s civil war was raging in Zimbabwe. On the main
campus in Harare blacks and whites ate meals separately. But in
the main refectory, black and white Christian students shared
meals together. In the midst of the increased tension this simple
testimony spoke powerfully. In silence, without preaching they
made a powerful demonstration of unity in Christ. First, the white
students served the main course to their black brothers and sisters;
then black leaders served the dessert to their white brothers and
sisters. This had a powerful impact in the university which was
affected by hostility and hatred between the two races. Their story
is still being told.

In the twenty-first century the power to reconcile people from different tribal and racial backgrounds will be a distinctive hallmark of the Christian gospel. We are pilgrims and our identity issues primarily from being in Christ and part of God's global family, the church, not from our birthplace. We must demonstrate that we have more in common with God's people from all nations than with non-Christians in our country of birth.

The university was affected by hostility and hatred between the two races.

In the history of IFES there has been a strong emphasis on the trans-racial, trans-cultural nature of Christian fellowship. From its early beginnings in the late 1970s, for example, the Israeli student movement emphasized that it was a fellowship of both Arabic-speaking believers and Hebrew-speaking believers in the country of Israel. This was perhaps demonstrated most powerfully in that all the General Secretaries of the student ministry in Israel have been Arabs, so from the minority racial grouping.

In addition, the two racial groups come together for national training events each year. This is not without difficulty. Few Hebrew-speaking students speak Arabic so as a gesture of brotherliness, Arabic-speaking students have consistently agreed to have many of the main talks in English (i.e. a third language) so that no particular language group is seen to have priority at such gatherings. Occasionally at student meetings they have also shared communion, as a visible expression of their oneness in Christ. True peace is when everyone is seeking what is best for the other side. Recognizing this fact, students from the Fellowship of Christian Students in Israel put up posters which read (in Hebrew and Arabic):

TRUE PEACE.
Yes it is possible!
It begins in the heart
Between man and God

A student newspaper once noted, 'Aziz is an Arab from a Christian family. Yosef is a Jew. Despite coming from two different worlds, their lives centre on a shared base, their faith in Jesus the Messiah.'

Over the years, IFES students have found themselves in some of the toughest crucibles of suffering. How has commitment to God's people transcended tribal and ethnic barriers?

The gospel in Rwanda's crucible

Rwanda is a small central African country with the highest population density in Africa, comprising 85% Hutu and 15% Tutsi. The Tutsis, largely a more privileged group with better education, used to reign. In 1962, this country achieved independence with a Hutu civilian government. But ethnic tension continued as a feature of life. With the assassination of President Habyarimana on his return from peace talks in Kenya on 6 April 1994, tension escalated to new proportions. The Hutu-led army massacred Tutsis mercilessly. The Tutsi dominant Rwanda Patriotic Front and Tutsi elements in the army fought back.

Masses of people fled the country, many dying from hunger and disease. Tutsi and Hutu violence immediately spilled into neighbouring Burundi.

As the news of the President's death circulated around Kigali, violence spread quickly. Antoine Rutayisiré, leader of the Rwanda IFES movement at that time, was caught up in it. Looking through the barricaded windows of his Kigali home he knew that in a few minutes he, his wife and two-year-old daughter would be dead. His heart missed a few beats then started pounding again.

'Oh God, protect me and my family,' Antoine whispered. Around 3.30pm he heard shouting. It grew nearer and nearer. He could see hand grenades and he looked through the window and saw a group of *Interhamwe* (Hutu extremist killers) at his gate. He could see their hand grenades and bloodstained machetes – eight to ten young men who were out to kill all ethnic Tutsis and any Hutus who were opposed to Rwanda's late president. Antoine was a Tutsi. His immediate neighbour was a Hutu and a local leader of the *Interhamwe*. Earlier that day he had heard his neighbour's son boast about the number of Tutsi and traitor Hutu he had killed (and the many sacks of francs that he had looted). How could Antoine and his family escape? He had been among the Christians in Kigali who had preached forgiveness and reconciliation for all ethnic groups. 'You are a traitor and sympathizer with the *Inkotanyi*. We shall deal with you.' A member of the *Interhamwe* had warned that these Christians stirred up meetings. (*Inkotanyi* are the mainly Tutsi rebel fighters of the Rwandan Patriotic Front who invaded Rwanda from neighbouring Uganda in October 1990.)

Fighting had broken out the night before at about the time the president's plane was shot down. By radio, the Ministry of Defence had instructed all civilians to stay indoors as there were troubles on the streets.

Antoine had locked the gate and all windows and doors of the house. His household prayed throughout the day. He could see young men looting and setting fire to the nearby hotel. 'I knew they would soon reach our house so we packed what we could, and kept money aside to give them in hope that they would leave us alone,' Antoine said.

At 3.35pm his gate was being shaken and banged. 'Should we break in or throw a hand grenade at the roof?' I heard someone say. Immediately wild and weird thoughts whirled in my mind at a flashing speed. 'Am I going to let them rape my wife, and kill my child before my very eyes? What type of death are we going die? Are they going to shoot us or cut us into pieces?' I shuddered. Then an idea came. 'Why don't you grab a stick and go out and fight them? Can't you die like a man?' This was a spontaneous, human reaction. I could recognize my own self as in the past I would never have tolerated ill treatment without fighting back. Memories from schooldays flashed in my mind from the 1973 Tutsi massacres.

Our resistance was rewarded then, but now I no longer had the inner will to fight. Then I remembered the promises the Lord had given during our morning prayers, 'He who dwells in the shelter of the Most High will rest in the shadow of the Almighty . . . I will say . . . The LORD, He is my refuge and my fortress, my God in whom I trust' (Psalm 91:1–2). I remembered other Bible verses that the Lord had given us the previous week, when I had to go preaching on one retreat and violence broke out when I was on the way: 'Have mercy on me, Oh God, have mercy on me, for in you my soul takes refuge. I will take refuge in the shadow of your wings until the disaster has passed' (Psalm 57:1). Then I felt my spirit growing calmer and I heard a quiet voice inside, telling me 'You have been preaching sermons on loving and praying for your enemies and now you want to die shedding blood. Instead of trying to die like a man why don't you just "die like a Christian?" ' I was deeply convicted in my heart as I remembered all the efforts I had made in the past to keep my heart pure of anger and bitterness. So I made this short prayer of confession: 'Lord, forgive me for thinking of making my own defence and give grace to obey you even to death. I ask for your blessing on these people and if it is your will that we die, have them give me time to die praying for them as you did on the cross.'

I remembered the promises the Lord had given during our morning prayers.

At that very moment a feeling of deep peace that I had never experienced before flooded through me, and I felt so light inside that a breeze could have swept me off the ground. I had accepted death and I knew what I would do when the killers came. Everything else did not matter anymore. I was ready to face death with a Christlike attitude and I was even curious to know how it feels after death.

But I did not find out that day, as no sooner had I finished sorting myself out inside that the staccato of the machine gun echoed down the street. The 'cockroaches' – a derisive name for RPF soldiers – shouted at the *Interhamwe* and they scattered across our compound and ran away down hill.

I never saw those 'liberators', as I just sat where I was. It had all lasted less than five minutes but it felt like a lifetime. The following days would be filled with horrendous scenes, but this episode was an invaluable preparation. That peace and spirit of forgiveness stayed with me even when I heard of the death of relatives and many close friends. It comforted me on the tiring road to exile, strengthened me through the hardships and poverty of life in a displaced persons camp. Such a close encounter with death gave me a new understanding, a new interpretation of the prophet's words:

> I will ransom them from the power of the grave;
>   I will redeem them from death.
> Where, oh death, are your plagues?
>   Where, oh grave, is your destruction?
> (Hosea 13:14)

For the next five days Antoine and his family stayed indoors and read the book of Revelation. They were not sure how many more days they would have on earth. On the sixth day a girl from the neighbourhood came with an RPF soldier and a mob of people with knives, clubs and machetes. They banged on his neighbour's door, broke it down and found the neighbour's wife and two children hiding.

They were not sure how many more days they would have on earth.

'Her husband killed all my family,' the girl shouted, pointing at the woman. The mob knifed her and all her children, piled mattresses on the dead bodies and set the house on fire. The smell of burning flesh was overpowering. Antoine and his family decided to flee with a few belongings and food to the Amahoro Stadium which was being protected by the United Nations forces. Only then did they discover everybody on the other side of their estate had been killed. For the following week, Antoine and his family camped on the stadium stairs and slept under the stars. The stadium itself was being bombed. One evening a bomb fell about ten metres from them. Thirty-five people died on the spot, fifty others were injured.

Soon the RPF decided it was too dangerous for the civilians. One evening the soldiers gave everyone ten minutes to pack what they could carry and prepare to leave. Antoine gathered together a few plantains, some clothes and cooking utensils. They trekked northwards from 9.00pm to 4.00am under the cover of darkness to a safer place. The following day they were evacuated to a town forty-five kilometres north of Kigali which was under RPF control.

The family was subsequently taken to a refugee camp. Antoine wrote at this time: 'I always said the Lord is good. But at times like this one realizes what that truly means. Many of my fellow Christian workers perished and I don't know where the others are. The Lord has snatched us out of hell and I am sure I still have some assignment to fulfil in this country.'

I wrote to him at the camp and offered to bring him out of the country to spend a year on sabbatical, resting and studying in Wales. I will never forget his reply. He was at that time sharing two rooms with his pregnant wife, Peninah, his daughter and several other people.

'Thank you for your kind offer. However, I must refuse your invitation. As soon as the way is open I must return to Kigali, for if I do not share my people's pain neither can I share with them the joy of the gospel.' Eventually he was able to return, and today he serves as the Director of Africa Enterprise, runs a ministry of reconciliation, and is Vice-Chairman of the National Committee for Peace and Reconciliation.

Israel Havigumana's costly endeavour

A year after the massacres I visited the work in Rwanda to try to understand what the student movement had gone through. Antoine had survived, but most other key leaders had perished, including Israel Havigumana and his family. Israel was a man who lived what he preached and he preached against ethnic hatred. In the 1972–73 massacres he had protected a Tutsi fellow student at the secondary school, covering him with his own body and receiving all the beating until he managed to get him out of reach of the attackers.

During the 1990–94 tensions that led to the genocide, Israel spearheaded a reconciliation ministry through a nationwide city crusade. But his friendships with Tutsi brothers and sisters were resented by the extremists and the Bible study group that met in his home was mistaken for RPF support meetings. In February 1994 a hand grenade was thrown into his home as a warning.

Antoine discussed with him the possibility of stopping their prayer group so as not to compromise his safety any longer. 'What Christian testimony would that be?' he retorted, 'to shy away from my brothers and sisters because they are targeted! I have been preaching reconciliation and I will live it even if I have to pay for it with my own blood.' Pay with his blood he did. He was gunned down the very first day of the massacres with his three daughters, Rachel, Danielle and Mirai, in the company of his father and some visitors. Danielle survived.

The tension was palpable in the days leading up to the massacres. Israel, Antoine and Tutsi and Hutu students had preached in the open air on the main campus in Butare that in Christ there is neither Hutu nor Tutsi, that we are one. As a result the students were hunted down in the first days of the massacre. I asked Antoine why we had lost so many key leaders. He said he felt they were targeted because they provided an articulate alternative voice to the voice of extremism. In the first forty-eight hours the extremists killed all the moderate politicians and then key

Christian student leaders. The movement was left almost leader-less as a result of the massacres.

Nevertheless, God has brought beauty out of the ashes in Rwanda. In 1996 when I was able to visit the movement again, the group in Butare had grown to 300 registered members, but at daily prayer meetings between 500 and 1,000 students came. The spiritual hunger on the campus was beyond description, even though life was very difficult.

Despite remarkable deliverance for some of God's people and the courage many students showed in Rwanda in these difficult times, a million people died in the genocide in a little over a hundred days – and thousands fled. A quarter of the population was lost, affecting every family in the land. This was a culmination of forty years of conflict between Hutus and Tutsis. It left over 350,000 orphans and thousands of widows. As many women were raped in the genocide, HIV/AIDS is widespread with 11% of the population infected.

How could this catastrophe have happened in such a pre-dominantly Christianized country? In the 1991 census over 90% of Rwandans called themselves Christians from either a Catholic or Protestant background. The country was deeply affected by the East African revival seventy years ago.

Roots of a new movement

By 2002, under the leadership of Phocas Ngendahayo, the reborn movement UGBR was able to host its first national camp. Over three hundred students took part and heard moving messages on our unity in Christ. Talks were deep, relevant, contextualized, challenging, equipping and visionary. During the conference around seventy of the students visited the site of the genocide at Murambi where 27,000 people were killed. 'It was a horrible and moving event,' wrote Phocas. They joined hands, Hutus and Tutsis together with friends from overseas, and prayed, 'Never let that happen again in Rwanda.' Some of them had family members killed there. On the way back to the campus, people reacted differently, some wept, others kept silent – others sang Christian songs of hope. Together they were united because of Christ.

Phocas is another of God's special servants lent to IFES. He was not yet married in 1994 and he and his immediate family were in the Congo; he lost all his wider family in Rwanda at that time, apart from one uncle. His future wife, Jackie, was living with her family in Rwanda throughout those months of terror. They now have three children: Jisca and twin sons who share the name Ebenezer: Eben and Ezer. What a testimony those boys' names will be all their lives – to the faith of their parents, and more, to the faithfulness of God. 'Right up to now the Lord has helped us.'[1]

Talks were deep, relevant, contextualized and visionary.

I was moved when a colleague told me of a conversation she had with Phocas. The movement had lost almost all the students, graduates and board. She mused that in rebuilding the work he must have had to start from nothing. As they were walking along the road, talking as they went, Phocas suddenly stopped. He was plainly surprised by her comment and perhaps even wondered if he had misheard. 'No,' he said, 'We didn't start from nothing. We had the Bible, the Holy Spirit and Christ's great commission'; then as if to take the point home he repeated, 'So we didn't start from nothing!' How we westerners need our African brethren to remind us of hope in the face of what would otherwise be dreadful hopelessness. Phocas is a man of hope.

In 2000, I invited Phocas to the UK for two terms of theological study at the Cornhill Training Course. When he returned, he took a deliberate step to strengthen the use of Scripture among students. He established a Bible study department to train Bible study leaders and equip them to train their members in handling

Scripture. The Norwegian movement raised the funds and the Kenyan movement provided the person for this role. It was a great IFES partnership. The 3,000 students who gather on a Saturday night in a sports stadium close to the University in Butare are not all Christians, but they have two things in common: each comes from a family left deeply traumatized by the genocide and all are drawn by the gospel's message of hope.

Phocas has seen that if the movement is to be strong it must be built on a deeper knowledge of Scripture than previous generations had. The major teaching conferences help here. In December 2005 the title of the conference was 'Raising up an Ezra Generation' – a generation of students and graduates who love Scripture will bring it into the nation's public life. Participants covenanted to read the Bible through in 2006, and asked us to ship over copies of the Murray McCheyne Reading Plan *More Precious than Gold*.[2]

Challenges in Burundi

The violence in Rwanda spilled over into Burundi where civil war ran on for years. In these difficult situations Emmanuel Ndikumana sought to keep the ministry together.

Once again, Hutu and Tutsi believers stood firm on the university campus in speaking and living for Christ. On one occasion fighting broke out on the campus. Over a dozen students were killed, mostly Hutus. Other Hutu students fled to the nearby mountains. They were followed by Tutsi Christians who took food and clothing, first to their brothers and sisters in Christ, but also to others. As a result some of the Tutsi Christian students were rejected by their families because they put their allegiance to believers ahead of their tribal allegiance and their allegiance to brothers and sisters in Christ before their families.

However, as news reached the principal of the university, who was not a believer, he said 'Our culture is disintegrating. On our campus there are three types of people: Hutus, Tutsis and Christians. If our culture is to survive, we must follow the example of the Christians.' Such a stand was not without its cost. Extremists condemned the Christian students and labelled them as traitors of their respective ethnic groups. Some were severely beaten or disowned by their families or even murdered because of their non-partisan stance.

At that time Emmanuel wrote, 'It is not easy to say what is going on here. It all depends on the one who says it. Some seem really tired and already pessimistic. Only a few remain optimistic. I am among the last ones doing everything I can to share the reasons for hope (founded on my faith in what God is saying in Scripture) with my brothers from the Christian Union. Their testimony is shining like many candles in a tempestuous wind. The miracle is that this light keeps shining, and can be seen from far off.'

If our culture is to survive, we must follow the example of the Christians.

In Burundi conflict occurred between students and the university administration over the exam timetable. Students went on strike and were sent home. In situations like this in the past, tensions had arisen quickly because of mistrust between ethnic and regional groupings. The national student leader, Edmond, a believer and a member of the GBU, spoke on all the private radio stations and explained the problem calmly. He met with the Minister for Education and the Parliament Commission for Social Affairs and won their confidence. As a result, the Minister for Education ruled in favour of the students. For the first time in years there was no ethnic or regional tension in the University of Bujumbura. Students and staff asked Edmond to reveal his 'secret'. Some said it would be wise to let all the student committee places go to GBU members. They said these people had given back honour and respect to academia in Burundi.

We thank God for the testimony of these brave brothers and sisters in Christ who stood publicly for gospel witness in trans-racial and trans-ethnic conflict. The catastrophe of the Rwandan and Burundi holocaust raises serious questions for the church in the twenty-first century, as indeed for student ministry. As we reflect on those terrible months, we must all ask questions about whether our own theology of race is firmly founded in Scripture, and how we can help to ground and nurture younger Christians in their understanding of racial identity.[3] May God help us grasp more and more deeply the glorious implications of our oneness in Christ, and of our deepest identity as being 'found in him'.

7 : The new Europe since 1989

Whatever time you phone, they're praying. If you ring in the morning, they're praying. If you ring in the afternoon, they're praying.
(said of the students in Samara, West Russia)

We see the impact of the gospel in Eastern Europe very powerfully following the fall of the Berlin Wall in 1989. As time passes it is easy for us to forget what an astonishing event this was, which freed more than thirty countries from the overpowering influence of communist ideology.

A remarkable work had existed among Russian students before the Russian Revolution, led by Vladimir Martinovsky.[1] After the Revolution it had come under severe pressure and in Moscow the student leaders introduced a new condition of membership for their group: to answer 'Yes' to the question: 'Are you willing to die for Christ?' The movement was eventually stamped out. This left little hope of evangelism in Russian universities for the next sixty years.

In the late 1980s things began to change. For years, universities in the USSR had drawn students from Africa, as fees were much lower there than in the West. The African Christians naturally talked with their Russian friends about Christ, and prayed for those friends. It was costly for them to be known as Christians, but many saw this cost as part of their discipleship. The KGB noted the names of the most active believers, often sending them home without a degree in the final year of a six-year course. What courage those Africans showed.[2]

Only a tiny part of the story of Soobshchestvo Studentov Kristian (CCX-Russia), now active in twenty cities from St Petersburg to the heart of Siberia, can be told here.[3] God was working out his purposes not only through Russian and African students but, from Autumn 1990, through teams of IFES graduates coming to help from Denmark, Syria, Croatia, the UK and North America.

A major university in St Petersburg had a special link with Finnish medical students and gave scholarships to them annually, reserving most places for Communist Party members. In 1989 three of the five extra places were taken by keen evangelicals who saw their strategic opportunity and did not waste it. Discovering each other, they asked for the use of the 'Red Corner' in their dormitory for a Bible study, and a group began. Marianne Babashkina, one of the Finns, helped arrange a city-wide gathering of Christian students. Soon over 100 were attending regularly. As time went on, an important feature here was a weekly all-city prayer meeting: students got into the habit, once church was over, of going to the team flat to eat and pray.

In October 1991 IFES placed a similar group of graduates in Moscow Linguistic University to learn Russian and be the aroma of Christ among the students. It was a remarkable time, with enormous interest in biblical Christianity because it had been banned for so long, and within a short time there were around a dozen groups of Russian students all studying the Bible.

In Nizhny Novgorod a fine group grew from an initiative of four Russian students. One was Igor Maskaev who became the first staff worker and was later appointed deputy governor to Boris

Nomtsev who was to become the next prime minister. The
Nizhny leaders had been Komsomol-trained and their abilities to
organize showed that training at its best. Olga Loukmanova, a
Nizhny graduate of that era, later joined the CCX staff taking
pastoral responsibility for the staff team across the whole of
western Russia. She recalls the way the Nizhny students worked
to bring the gospel to their university:

> One Christmas an American staffworker felt so homesick that she
> baked a plateful of pancakes, took along two Russian students
> (brand new Christians), quickly taught them a few Christmas carols,
> and walked around the dorm knocking on doors, singing carols for
> people, handing out pancakes and candy and saying 'Merry
> Christmas' to whoever would open the door.
>
> On another occasion we held an evangelistic meeting at a local
> McDonalds. Again we were helped by Americans. A team of visiting
> evangelists paid for 100 meals, and we asked Christian students to
> come for a free meal as long as they could bring a non-believing friend
> with them. We did this twice or three times. It was a way of reaching
> a large group of non-Christians. By that time (it must have been
> around 1997–98) the novelty of Christian preaching had worn off, so
> the best way to ensure attendance seemed to be the magnet of food!

Amid the chaos of the early post-Soviet years, there were many
opportunities to let Christian students hear of the vision right
across the mighty land mass. Olga toured with her American
colleague Dan Wynard through several parts of the CIS, speaking
of CCX and drawing students into it. Some students they met were
already taking very imaginative initiatives; one group was working
on a musical based around an evangelistic booklet produced by
Campus Crusade for Christ! The first all-Russia conference was
held in January 1992, with 100 students from about sixteen cities.
Victor Avdeev, one of the speakers, wept as he looked at his
student audience. Back home in St Petersburg he had attempted
outreach to the student Atheists' Club, with a real sense of fear

because evangelicals had been excluded from Soviet intellectual circles for so long. A Christian student movement had seemed an impossible dream.

And yet now that dream was coming true in many parts of the former USSR. In 1991 Pete Lowman, a graduate of Cardiff University in the UK, visited the Belarussian capital Minsk and drew audiences of several hundred students, preaching the gospel with the deputy rector by his side! Of course there was an attraction in seeing someone from a formerly-banned nation speaking on a formerly-banned topic! But there was huge interest in the Christian faith: a sense that the old certainties were gone, that there was a major collapse of the old ethical framework, that something new and different was needed to rebuild the nation and rebuild community.

Within a year or two, however, this interest was waning. There were several reasons. The economic situation was bad; life could be very hard; and in general Western influence tended to promote acquisitive materialism, and, as Jesus said, it's easier for a camel to go through a needle's eye than for someone with that sort of mentality to enter the kingdom of heaven! Also, there had been such a flood of Western religious salesmen – every kind of cult and denomination, the good the bad and the ugly – and people became tired of it. Finally, after the profound sense of national humiliation associated with the collapse of communism, there was an inevitable resurgence of nationalism; and in that context evangel-icalism was often perceived as a Western import, with the Orthodox Church doing all it could to restrict it, leading in both Russia and Belarus to the passing of a strong anti-Protestant, anti-missionary law.

Despite all this the student work continued to grow. In 1995 IFES was invited by Baptists in Samara to bring a small team to that city. One pastor there had been expelled from university during the war for witnessing to a room-mate; he had longed and prayed for the day when a Christian group could meet in the university. God was at work even before the team arrived, as two

Russian students started a prayer meeting. Indeed Samara was to become known as a student group where 'Whatever time you phone, they're praying. If you ring in the morning, they're praying. If you ring in the afternoon, they're praying.' The team kept an 'open flat' which was always full of students, and very soon an able group of Russian student leaders emerged, and the IFES team was able to leave.

In the second half of the 1990s CCX became more established. It was officially registered in January 1996 in Nizhny. The strong presence of Nizhny CCX graduates who would continue to support the work made it an obvious choice of place to register. A year later Natasha Stepanova became the first Russian General Secretary, making it a completely Russian-led movement. And with the growing maturity of the evangelical churches across the country, more students were able to take initiatives in a way few had dared earlier. New groups were now emerging in far-flung places like Krasnoyarsk, Chelyabinsk, Izhevsk and Voronezh.

Whatever time you phone, they're praying.

Moving accounts of forgiveness

Pavel Raus, an early leader in the Czech Republic, comments on events immediately following the fall of the communist system:

> A gathering in the centre of Prague drew tens of thousands. All of a sudden two policemen came to the stage. A few days earlier they had been beating students, and now publicly asked forgiveness. The whole crowd started to pray the Lord's Prayer ... 'Forgive us our debts as we also forgive our debtors.' I could not believe it. Can you imagine! After forty years of atheist ideology, after forty years of persecution of Christians, after forty years of systematic teaching of a materialistic

world-view in all the schools, after forty years of aggressive communist propaganda, the whole nation prays the Lord's Prayer.

At a similar meeting in Bratislava, two women came to the stage. Both had lost daughters who had been shot by Russian soldiers in 1968. These girls had become symbols of oppression because they had been killed in front of the university. Their mothers said they were prepared to forgive the Russians and they asked all students standing there to forgive them as well. We all began repeating quietly 'We forgive, we forgive.' You could hear it from everywhere. I was crying, and I was not the only one. A big burden of hatred was somehow taken from us. 'Forgive us our debts as we also have forgiven our debtors, because then we can be really free.'

Allow me to share stories which highlight the power of the gospel to transform lives in post-Soviet Georgia.

Georgia is a complex nation. It officially converted to Christianity in AD 337 and there has always been a strong Georgian Orthodox Church in spite of many years under Islamic occupation. But it has been a watered down Christian faith, poorly understood and mixed liberally with superstition and animism. However, there are historical precedents of wonderful times of renewal and revival.

In the 1990s it was common for students to gather together from the three Caucasian nations, even during times of conflict between Armenia and Azerbaijan over the territory of Nagorno-Karabakh. At one conference two students from these countries embraced and prayed for each other and their nations, expressing joy and amazement at how Jesus had transformed their hearts. Barrett Horne, IFES Regional Secretary, told me the story:

As they stood with their arms around each others' shoulders in warm affection, I thought of how their nations remain in a state of war, each painting the other in draconian terms. Both these men had served in their national armies and might easily have faced each other in combat. Their expression of brotherly love and friendship in Christ was still potentially dangerous, were it to become known to their communities. So it took considerable courage. Yet here they were, embracing as brothers and serving as leaders within the growing Christian student movements that have taken root in their countries.

This openness to forgive and resolve to build a really new people, not in the Marxist sense but in the biblical sense, has characterized the new student movements in former Soviet states all across Eurasia. In this context, the student work began to grow in Georgia in the early 1990s as indeed it did in neighbouring Armenia and Azerbaijan.

A grandson at the graveside

At one conference, a student arrived for the meeting on the last day in tears. Leaders asked what was wrong. 'I always believed Christians hate Muslims and sometimes kill them. But you have loved me,' he said.

Arriving back home, he told his Muslim father he had become a Christian. 'Do you mean that seriously?' his father asked, 'Yes', he replied. 'Then let's talk about it again in a few weeks.' True to his word, his father asked the same question the following month and received the same reply. Not long afterwards the student's grandfather died. In traditional fashion his body was placed on a bier in the house and hundreds of friends came for six days to express condolence and show their honour. On the seventh day everyone processed to the burial site.

The threat of danger could not keep this student silent.

With astonishing courage, the nineteen-year-old began to address everyone as they stood around the grave: 'My grandfather was a Muslim, my father is a Muslim and I have been a Muslim. I searched the Koran but I couldn't find salvation in it. Now at my grandfather's graveside I want to tell you all that I have read the gospel and found salvation in Christ. How I wish that you could all believe in Jesus.' The threat of danger could not keep this student silent. There was a complete hush. No-one dared touch him.

Crossing the border

Another story was related by Lena, staff of CCX-Ukraine. On the way from the Ukraine to Azerbaijan, she and a small mission team of three girl students encountered a situation far worse than they could have imagined. It was a terrifying journey.

The train had to pass through the war-scarred semi-autonomous Russian republic of Chechnya where tens of thousands have been killed through their desperate rebellion against Russian rule, with kidnappings of soldiers and civilians almost daily. From the train windows students looked out on scenes of destruction.

At the Chechnya border, guards joined the train to accompany them until the Azeri frontier. There were many searches and document checks. At one station a man dressed as a guard burst into the compartment. Standing menacingly with his weapon he ordered everyone but Lena out, and then demanded to see all the money she was carrying. Lena felt she had no choice but to reveal what she had – the money for the whole team, to cover all their expenses. He took it and ran out and off the train. The guards came running and tried to find him, but he had escaped. Their comfort was to tell Lena that she was fortunate not to have been raped or killed. You can imagine how she felt.

Gradually the Chechnyan guards became intrigued by this foolish group of Ukrainian students passing through such danger- ous territory. Conversations developed and slowly they and the mission team became human beings to each other, people with names and families. Students took pictures of their new friends.

The friendship proved valuable. At one checkpoint, a student was nearly dragged off the train. He was a Russian studying at the seminary in Ukraine, and his passport was said to lack some kind of stamp to prove that he was not avoiding conscription. The now friendly Chechnyan train guards prevented him from being taken into custody.

The team had a wonderful and fruitful mission in Azerbaijan, but always there was the dread of having to return through Chechnya. When the day came to depart, a large group of Azeri students saw them off, weeping and thanking God for the encouragement they had been to each other, grateful for the vision shared with Ukrainian students.

With trepidation they came to the Chechnyan border, receiving the guards who would accompany them. To their surprise and relief the team was joined by the same guards who had travelled down with them! Moreover they brought food and prepared a feast for the students. The guards were delighted when the students gave them copies of the photos they had taken on the way down. As the evening wore on, the team began to sing for the guards, sharing with them the Christian songs that mean so much to the CCX students.

The guards being Muslims were first taken aback and unsure about these Christian songs – but gradually relaxed and entered into the spirit of the singing. The climax came as they were singing a song about the unconditional love of God. That song seemed to break the heart of one soldier who began to weep. Here was a tough, no doubt battle-hardened Chechnyan soldier, an AK47 rifle at his side, and tears running down his cheeks. 'We are not all bad people. Please tell your friends that we are not all bad people,' the guard pleaded.

We do not know the ultimate impact of the CCX student mission team on those Chechnyan soldiers, but we are confident that the Lord was present from start to finish and believe that some seeds of the gospel were planted as students shared their faith, their love of Jesus and their own lives with those soldiers.

The former Yugoslavia

Yugoslavia was formed after the First World War from areas that had been either independent or part of the Ottoman or Austro-Hungarian empires. Ethnic conflicts were apparent right from the beginning. It was a monarchy, then a republic. Then overrun by the Germans in the Second World War it became a communist state under Marshall Tito.

Yugoslavia was a united country in one thing at least, that Soviet tanks should not roll into its capital. This fear was always strong enough to unite it until the collapse of the Soviet Union. Yugoslavia was then split into six republics and two autonomous provinces under Tito: Bosnia Herzegovina, Croatia, Macedonia, Montenegro, Serbia, Slovenia, Kosova and Vojvodina.

Loyalties had always been complicated because inter-marriage and mobility meant there were Serbs living in Croatia, Croats living in Serbia, Bosnian Muslims living in Serbia and Croatia, Serbs and Croats living in Bosnia – and so on. Through fear of aggression, those from mixed marriages were forced to declare for one side or the other, which made for great pain within families.[4]

Students faced stark choices in how to relate across the ethnic divide.

IFES has been involved in the area from the beginning of the 1980s. Following the fall of the Berlin Wall, as events began to unravel in Yugoslavia, hostilities broke out, and many students faced stark choices in how to relate to their brothers and sisters in Christ across the ethnic divide. In 1992 the General Secretaries of both the Serbian and Croatian student movements attended an IFES staff consultation in Eastern Europe. Dan Denk, IFES Regional Secretary, wrote:

> It was their first opportunity to meet since the war with Croatia had started. They had some heated discussions and shared stories. We

just let them talk and work through it. The next time I looked they were praying together for one another's countries, and for peace. They were able to set aside divisions and affirm one another as brothers in Christ.

It is this emphasis on seeing themselves as Christian first, and Serb / Croat / Bosnian second, that Dan felt was essential.

At the European Evangelism Conference over Easter 1994 in Warsaw, students from Croatia and the new Yugoslavia (former Serbia and Montenegro) formed a joint choir to sing at an evening prayer concert. Through the conference they were frequently seen together and they wept when they were separated for their journey home. They might not have agreed on the causes of war between their countries, but they were united in their purpose of promoting reconciliation.

As the country disintegrated, and Kosovo broke away, many crossed the border into the Republic of Macedonia, which had a population of only two million. This was swelled by 300,000 Kosova Albanian refugees. Kosta Milkov, then staff worker of the young Macedonian student movement, told me that Macedonians largely considered Albanians as 'enemy'. Through the efforts of Macedonian Christians, many refugees found Christ during that time declaring simply, 'We have been overwhelmed by love.'

In January 2000, Christian students gathered together for a great concert of peace in Skopje, with a choir of Albanians and Serbs. They sang a song composed by Josip, a student leader from Belgrade. The chorus ran:

Then the lion and the lamb will lie down together,
God will take away all tears and pain,
There will not be wars and death,
That will be the real country of love.

Everyone clapped and many started to cry because of the powerful presentation of unity and love. 'Some people did not believe

Albanians would sing with the Serbian choir. But they saw it with their own eyes! It is not surprising that many of us were weeping.'

Another participant wrote thoughtfully, 'We are happy to take part and to see this mixed choir. It was really bad during the conflict. Six members of my family are dead but the Lord gave me strength and I prayed for my brethren in Serbia. I also prayed for President Milosovic for he needs salvation as well. Only by faith can we live together in peace. We have to be an example to people by our love and support for each other. It is not easy to come and sing together, but we *can* do it.'

During the NATO air attacks on Belgrade, Guta, a staff worker was with a group of thirty to forty students and others about to share Communion:

> As we met, sirens announced another air attack. What should we do? Leave and take shelter, or stay? The dilemma was quickly resolved. Children were taken into a basement and the service continued. 'This is my body, which is for you.' The Spirit stirred hearts. As the bread and wine were distributed, we were sharing fellowship with Christ. Outside human faces resembled Munch's painting 'The Scream'. But the Lord was with his chosen people in a real way. As God's people were swallowing the bread and wine their faces started to change, first into shy smiles, then into joy and laughter.
>
> In the midst of suffering the Lord brought joy and love. People stayed to encourage one another, delaying their departure into the world of silence and detonations. What stayed with them as a treasure was the broken body of our Lord Jesus. May this broken body bind us all, Serbs and Americans, people from Niç and Scotland, people from Novi Sad and from the Netherlands, from Belgrade and France. One died for many so that all may live. We may disagree on how to resolve the Balkan knot, but one thing brings us together: Christ's blood shed for us.

We look to God for people of his choice to lead the student work forward in these countries which have known such brokenness.

Noisy quiet times

One of the greatest joys of student ministry is discipling young Christians, like the Ukrainian student at the conference who had not heard of Daniel. Enjoy this heartwarming account from Krisztina Toth, a Hungarian staffworker invited to bring Bible expositions to a conference in the Caucasus:

> When you've been in IFES as long as I have, you expect people to spend their 'quiet time' alone and quietly before God. I'd been asked to prepare questions for the students to have their own quiet times following the Bible teaching. But I began to wonder why.
>
> Most of us stayed near the stove, as it was very cold in the building. The noise level didn't drop. It seemed these students had no idea of personal study or prayer. Had they been listening? Did they want to grow spiritually? I felt discouraged.
>
> Then I started to watch. I didn't understand what they were saying, but suddenly I realized the 'older' Christians (who had been converted a year or so) were explaining things to those who came to faith just weeks – or days – before!
>
> They showed them how to approach a book of the Bible they had never read before; how to apply it to their own lives; how to pray in the light of what they had just read – what 'quiet time' *really* means.
>
> As the week went on, I saw more and more clearly that they are learning to understand Paul's words better than I do: to share with him in his sufferings, and not to be ashamed of the gospel. They were beginning to see that following Christ would not make them popular, maybe not even accepted – possibly despised.
>
> As the 'quiet time' finished I sensed that the quiet place where the Lord speaks – in me and in them – had grown a little. I'm starting to understand why there's a celebration in heaven.

We are living in unusual times when we have greater opportunity for the gospel in more countries in the world than the church has ever had before. To invest in the lives of first-generation new Christians who themselves are already investing in the lives of younger converts is an urgent privilege.

8 : The call to sacrifice

Sacrifice is the badge of discipleship.
(Dietrich Bonhoeffer)

And what more shall I say? I do not have time to tell about Gideon,
Barak, Samson, Jephthah, David, Samuel and the prophets, who through
faith conquered kingdoms, administered justice, and gained what was
promised; who shut the mouths of lions, quenched the fury of the
flames, and escaped the edge of the sword; whose weakness was turned
to strength; and who became powerful in battle and routed foreign
armies. Women received back their dead, raised to life again. Others
were tortured and refused to be released, so that they might gain a better
resurrection. Some faced jeers and flogging, while still others were
chained and put in prison. They were stoned; they were sawed in two;
they were put to death by the sword. They went about in sheepskins and
goatskins, destitute, persecuted and ill-treated – *the world was not worthy
of them*. They wandered in deserts and mountains, and in caves and holes
in the ground. These were all commended for their faith, yet none of
them received what had been promised. God had planned something
better for us so that only together with us would they be made perfect.
(Hebrews 11:32–40, my italics)

The Russian writer Tolstoy once wrote, 'Whoever wants an easy life was born in the wrong generation.' Without sacrificial service it is impossible to conceive of the growth of a work of God. That kind of service was the central thrust of Howard Guinness's book, *Sacrifice*, first published in 1936. He wrote:

> Where are the young men and women of this generation who will hold their lives cheap, and be faithful even unto death, who will lose their lives for Christ's, flinging them away for love of him? Where are those who will live dangerously, and be reckless in his service? Where are the men of prayer? Where are the men who count God's Word of more importance to them than their daily food? Where are the men who, like Moses of old, commune with God face to face as a man speaks with his friend? Where are God's men in this day of God's power?

The verses quoted above from Hebrews 11 show that sacrificial service was part of the call to follow the God of the Bible. This key passage highlights several principles:

- *The Christian life is a battle.* Paul Negrut, leader of the Baptist church in Oradea, Romania, with over 3,000 members and a youth group of 800, once wrote, 'The Christian life is not a game but a battle. There is no blessing without sacrifice.' The Old Testament stories recounted in Hebrews 11 highlight this truth; all through Christian history, including the history of student ministry, spiritual battles have had to be fought for the work of God to go forward.
- *Hardship is common for those in Christian service* (vv. 35–38). Discipleship can be costly at many levels. For some, especially those who work cross-culturally, it means having to give up cultural privileges. The people we go to serve will be unconcerned by the prestigious university we studied at, or the level of degree we attained. It does not matter to them whether we had a first-, second- or third-class degree,

or even a doctorate. Many cross-cultural workers who have graduated from some of the best universities around the world have found that hard.

Sacrifice may involve accepting a lower standard of living. I remember the beginnings of the Yugoslavian student movement in the early 1980s when the communist system still held sway, before the dramatic civil war of the 1990s. Student ministry began in Zagreb and spread to Belgrade and two or three other cities. After a while, we were able to employ the first part-time student worker, Stevan Madjarac. Stevan, a Serb, and his wife Nina, a Croat, were married during the first European Evangelism Conference in Holland in 1985. They clearly saw that IFES crossed all barriers of ethnicity, and were expressing their commitment to this. Stevan was an able student who was then employed to teach part-time at his local university. Unfortunately, news of his involvement with student ministry came to the attention of the university authorities. He was called in for a meeting with senior staff. They challenged him, saying they wished to promote him to a full-time teaching position, but could do so only if he give up links with the student ministry. He refused to do this, and found himself relieved of his part-time teaching job. He had paid a price, but his example inspired others to serve with the ministry – and it has grown wonderfully. Stevan now works as an agronomist with the United Nations. This early experience in his Christian life was a salutary lesson in the costliness of standing firm for the gospel.

Another outstanding example of a young graduate prepared to give up a potentially lucrative lifestyle to serve students is Vinoth Ramachandra of Sri Lanka. Vinoth completed a doctorate at London University in the 1970s. As a nuclear engineer he was offered attractive positions in the USA. Passionately committed to his home country and disturbed by the brain drain of many Sri Lankans who were lured to the States, he declined. Instead he accepted an invitation from IFES to become the first student worker in Sri Lanka. He later became General Secretary of the student movement and went on to serve IFES with distinction as Regional Secretary for South Asia for many years. All this time Vinoth received a minimal salary because he wanted to be paid at the same level as local workers. He sacrificed considerable financial advantage for the cause of the gospel. Vinoth still serves with IFES. He and his wife Karin continue to be based in Colombo.

Risking the loss of security and health

In the late 1980s the Fellowship needed someone to start student ministry in Mozambique, south-east Africa. The country had just come out of a civil war which had lasted almost as long as the one that had wrecked Angola. Chua Wee Hian searched around the world for someone to go there, but his efforts seemed fruitless, until he came across Samuel Johnson. Samuel, from the USA, had spent many years in Brazil in literature ministry. He and his wife Corinne offered to go to Mozambique.

I was deeply impressed when I heard of Samuel's vision and preparedness to sacrifice for the gospel. He was in his mid-fifties. When I met him three years later, he told me he had been through more emotional ups and downs in that time than in the rest of his life put together. But his eyes lit up as we talked, 'The University of Maputo has only four thousand students. If with God's help I can establish a strong student witness there, I believe we can influence the direction of the government and church life in the entire country. That is what keeps me going.' He was a modern-day Caleb. Shortly afterwards, Samuel died from cerebral malaria. He died reaching for the goal. Impressed by his testimony, others have followed on in seeking to build student ministry since then.

A remarkable female staff worker in the history of IFES is Tonica van der Meer. Tonica is Brazilian, with family links to the Netherlands going back several generations. She served first in the Brazilian movement and then in war-torn Angola for over a decade. When I became Regional Secretary for Europe, the student work in Portugal was struggling with barely fifteen to twenty students attending annual conferences. We desperately needed a gifted Bible study trainer to help strengthen the work. Tonica had come to All Nations Christian College in England for a two-year cross-cultural missions course. I visited to plead with her to serve with IFES in Portugal. She had significant experience in Brazil and spoke Portuguese – an ideal background. However, she politely declined. She had skin cancer, and had been warned by doctors not to live in a hot country where she would expose her skin to the sun's rays.

Several years later, I heard that Tonica had gone to Angola as the first student worker there. Angola was in the midst of a brutal civil war, which lasted over two decades following the departure of the Portuguese colonial government in the early 1970s. When I next met her I asked why she had gone to Angola given that the climate was much hotter than in Portugal. Surely this would be difficult for her skin problem. 'The Lord called me,' she said, 'so I couldn't resist.' I knew she had been engaged at college, so I asked what happened to her fiancé. 'He didn't want to come,' she said, 'so I ended the relationship.'

We desperately needed a gifted Bible study trainer.

After ten years in Angola, Tonica wrote to me:

In Luanda and Lubango there is some sort of normality. But this is an exception. We see no progress in reaching a peace agreement. The economy has collapsed. Food, water, medicine have become rare and expensive. People are dying from cholera and malaria. The official cemeteries are completely insufficient and there are many unofficial ones, some with more than 6,000 graves in a few months. Many people, even Christians, have lost hope. But when

I show them verses which encourage us to hope and pray there is a good response.

Several years later, peace came at last to Angola. I talked with Tonica at the time of her departure when she handed over to Angolan national leaders. She reflected on her years in the country, where life was characterized by corruption, lack of water, bombs and widespread casual violence. 'Angolans are by nature happy, but the long war and its aftermath have made them a very sad and broken people,' she said.

The war had far-reaching effects on the campus. Many male students were taken away from university to join the government forces, leaving more women studying than men, astonishing for an African country. Tribal divisions played a big part in the civil war, but here, as in other places benighted by strife, Christian students from different tribes overcame these barriers. When Christian students were called up, it was very painful.

Christian students from different tribes overcame these barriers.

Christians struggled with corruption as much as anyone. Some fell back into questionable activities, but generally wanted to try again. Tonica started a 'chain of honesty', to help students refuse to consent to corruption. If they could travel honestly, they would travel, but, if not, they would not. Those who committed themselves to this urged church members to do the same. They prayed for one another and felt a sense of accountability to one another in these things.

'God often uses suffering to bring people to himself and to work deeply in their lives,' said Tonica. To help students grasp this, her priority was for them to read the Bible with understanding, and to apply it in daily life. 'I kept teaching inductive Bible study, prayer and discipleship. These basic things are vital.'

Risking the loss of family and friends

One of the most outstanding IFES leaders in North Africa and the Middle East came from a strong Muslim background. Several of his family were members of a radical Islamic group and imprisoned for their beliefs. In the mid-1980s he came to study architecture in Paris. While there, he heard a series of lectures by a remarkable Muslim apologist, Chawkat Moucarry, who had a unique ability to relate the gospel to Muslims.

Chawkat had a passionate love for Muslims and Arabs especially, having been born in Syria, and could clearly explain to them the uniqueness of Christ. With degrees in Islamic studies and theology he was well equipped to do so. A man of strong convictions, he could remain calm even when hostile Muslim students provoked him. He could see beyond their reaction and felt a deep-seated compassion for them. He is the most remarkable apologist and evangelist I have seen in the Arabic-speaking world.

Our friend from North Africa came each evening. He approached Chawkat at the end of a lecture and asked if he could take a Gospel away with him. About six months after he returned home to North Africa, having read the Scriptures on his own, he became a Christian. He had heard there was a graduate of the French GBU in his home city and he made contact. They began meeting to study the Bible. After a few weeks, one of his older brothers became suspicious and followed him. This had a painful outcome.

His brothers set him an ultimatum. If he did not give up his new-found faith within one week, they would tell their father. He left home immediately, but was soon to hear of death threats from members of the Islamic movement.

Knowing of an international church in the city, he went there for help; the Swiss pastor got him out of the country within twenty-four hours, flying him to Switzerland to stay with relatives who were farmers in the Swiss Alps. This was in January 1987.

In a cold climate, surrounded by people he did not know, he started to wonder what he had done. The family managed to get him across the border to France and he returned to Paris, where he knew a few Christians. Chawkat took him in and cared for him. Later he told me that it was the love, compassion and community of Christians in Paris that were the means God had used to attract him to the gospel. He went on to study theology in Paris and began a ministry amongst Muslim friends, first in Paris, then more widely in France and later in the Middle East. In the early years in Paris, he wrote to his family through friends in Canada, fearful that if his brothers found out where he was, they might try to kill him. Fourteen years later he was able to visit his home country. By this time God had given him a wife and children. He has now been able to visit his family in North Africa two or three times, but they still know little of his ministry.

Risks in travel

There is always some element of risk in travel, but in some areas of the world the risk is much higher with real dangers of rebel fighting, robbery and hijack. The staff of our national movements are not naïve about this. Around the world each year, IFES staff and the staff of our national movements cover many thousands of miles in our commitment to serve students on their campuses.

Fidèle Mushidi was a staff worker in the Democratic Republic of Congo, based in the eastern region, near the Rwanda border. Daniel Bourdanné sent an email shortly after meeting him. It says everything of the man's courage and vulnerability:

> Fidèle is doing a wonderful job in difficult circumstances. On his way back from visiting one student group, rebels attacked his bus. They dragged him out and a rebel held a gun against him, threatening to shoot him. Mercifully, God intervened. The rebel was on the point of firing when another rebel – whom Fidèle had known as a

student – stopped him because of kindness Fidèle had shown him in the past. Eventually, they allowed the bus to go on its way.

Grace Morillo, General Secretary of the UCU in Colombia, served first on its staff as a campus worker. On a return flight from Bucaramanga to Bogotá in 1999, her plane was hijacked by terrorists:

Suddenly men were shouting: 'Hands up! Face the front! Keep your heads down and don't look up!' I began praying very hard, asking God to preserve lives, and especially to preserve the pilot. I started praying in tongues; other words wouldn't come. As I prayed I felt more and more at peace. I felt that the Lord was allowing it for a purpose.

After a rough landing on a slippery jungle airstrip, we were taken up river in small boats. Then came a five-hour, very fast car drive on dirt roads and through creeks where the water was really high. I was very angry at the guerrillas all day, not speaking to them or looking at them. But at that night's resting place, they gave us mattresses and told us they were going to respect our lives. They tried to keep our hopes up by telling us it was going to be fine.

Early on the sick and elderly were released and thirty-two of us went on, walking through farm areas, jungle areas and creeks for four or five hours a day. I began to talk to the guerrillas. When I mentioned the Lord to one lad of about fifteen or sixteen, he asked, 'Are you a Catholic?' Hearing I was an evangelical, he told me his parents were evangelicals, but he had not seen them for two years.

We soon got to know everyone in the group and we appointed organizers as the average person doesn't know how to live in community. We made sure everyone would at least have the basics and that we all had one another's names and phone numbers so anyone who was released could contact the others' families. We decided not to wear the clothes the guerrillas gave us, in case we got caught in crossfire, opting instead for extra clothes we had in our hand luggage.

One night a branch crashed down and I thought it was gunfire. I felt a type of fear I had never experienced, except in dreams. It wasn't the fear of dying but the fear of how it was going to happen. I took a lot of convincing that it was just a branch.

A priest, a nun and I started a daily prayer time at 6.30pm. Everyone's need of God was so evident and the prayer time became like fountains of water. Eventually we were split into smaller groups and my group of nine kept the prayer time. There was always a reason for thanksgiving, enough to keep us hopeful. Sometimes the guerrillas joined us. Once we all shared the peace together, including the guerrillas. Sometimes there were difficulties in the group, but the only way we could wish peace to one another was because of Jesus.

The hijacking took place on 12 April and Grace was released on 18 June. Less than a month later she travelled to South Korea to be at the IFES World Assembly, where she expressed her thanks for many prayers on her behalf. She had been surprised and humbled to learn that people all around the world had been praying for her. Grace reflected further on her experience:

It was evident from early on that it had nothing to do with us. Colombia is going through that kind of situation and believers are going to be touched by it. I was conscious of my weaknesses: the night before the hijacking, the Lord had called me to pray, but being tired, I didn't take out my Bible and didn't have it with me in my hand luggage. In spite of my weaknesses, God is still calling me, calling all of us, to commit ourselves to the reality around us. The guerrillas are very needy people, people who haven't known true and unconditional love. They see the world only through the small prism of their reality and they cannot conceive of another reality. They will probably die young. We need to learn how to build peace in our country and to be peacemakers. Mine was a benign type of suffering, a benign type of kidnapping. Others have suffered far more.

✣ ✣ ✣

We can be encouraged that we do not experience all the above difficulties at the same time! However, Paul's exhortation to Timothy still stands in 2 Timothy 2:3–4: 'Endure hardship with us like a good soldier of Christ Jesus. No-one serving as a soldier gets involved in civilian affairs – he wants to please his commanding officer.'

As we return to the passage in Hebrews 11, we notice a *third* key principle, in vv. 35–38. Not all believers serving the Lord wholeheartedly will be delivered from their difficulties. Earlier in the passage we read of people being delivered from trials, but in these three verses there is a change of emphasis. The mark of great faith is not deliverance but fidelity in the midst of difficulties. How we need this message today. One of the major heresies of recent times is prosperity theology, that God will financially prosper and keep in good health those who serve him fruitfully. Hebrews 11 does not teach that.

> *The mark of great faith is not deliverance but fidelity.*

Some proponents of prosperity theology believe that long-term suffering or difficulties must be due to a Christian's sinfulness or lack of faith. Though some of our problems *are* due to sin, Scripture teaches that others come from engagement in a spiritual battle, or simply because we are living in a fallen world. We cannot be exempt from these difficulties.

Let me illustrate. Professor Sir Norman Anderson was a man of towering intellect.[1] He lectured in Egypt, and was then Director of the Advanced Legal Institute at London University. He had a searing mind and could be devastating in debate. For over sixty years he supported the ministry of IFES. I was with him at one of the last public events at which he spoke. It was at a large conference for students in England with nearly 2,000 present.

During that meeting, he was interviewed by an Anglican curate in his late twenties. At that time, Professor Anderson's wife had senile dementia and she could no longer recognize him. All three of his children had died in early adulthood. I was taken aback by the curate's question. As he turned to Prof. Anderson, he said, 'When you look back over your life and reflect on the fact that you have lost all your three children, and now your wife of sixty years no longer recognizes you, do you ever ask the question, "Why me?"' It was a bold if not insensitive question. I was surprised by Professor Anderson's response. 'No, I've never asked the question, "Why me?" but I have asked the question, "Why not me?" I am not promised as a Christian that I will escape the problems encountered by others; we all live in a fallen world.

'When a plane goes down, there are sometimes Christians in it. Believers suffer from cancer, just as unbelievers do. I am not promised, simply because I am a Christian, that I will be delivered from all difficulties in this world. I am, however, promised that in the midst of difficulties, God through Christ will be present with me, and will give his grace to help me cope with the difficulties and bear witness to him.'

He seemed to be echoing Paul in Philippians 1 where the apostle speaks of rejoicing in Christ even from the darkness of a prison cell. Prosperity theology seems to lack a theology of suffering and has an inadequate eschatology, for most of the promises given to us in the Bible are fulfilled only beyond death. We have to look at those promises with the eye of faith. That is why Paul could write 'For to me, to live is Christ and to die is gain' (Philippians 1:21).

'Of whom the world is not worthy'

Let me share with you some examples of people of whom the world was not worthy (v. 38), who have been engaged in student ministry, standing in the midst of opposition and, in some cases, losing their lives.

First, to Ethiopia. In the 1980s the Ethiopian people lived under the yoke of a very repressive communist regime led by President

Mengistu. Thousands of Christians lost their lives because of their faith, yet, at the same time, the church grew rapidly. When I visited the country in 1996 after the fall of the communist system, I heard that at least 200,000 people had been added to the church each year for the previous six years. When I questioned my host about the reasons for this, he said it was because of leaders who had stood firm in their commitment to Christ in the face of hostile opposition.

He told me the story of a pastor who was a giant in all senses of the word. He was 6ft 8in. tall, and a great preacher, imprisoned under the Mengistu regime. He was such an important figure that church leaders appealed to President Nyerere, from Tanzania, to bring pressure on the Ethiopian government for his release. President Nyerere agreed and travelled in his personal jet to Addis Ababa, asking the Ethiopian Foreign Secretary if, as a personal favour, he would release this pastor. The favour was granted. The pastor was duly brought to the Tanzanian Embassy; from here he would travel by limousine with President Nyerere to his plane and then be whisked out of the country.

Leaders had stood firm in the face of hostile opposition.

At the Embassy President Nyerere greeted him. 'Today you are going to be set free. You will leave the country with me.' But the pastor stopped him saying, 'No, I am not leaving the country. My place is here. If I leave, it will discourage all those pastors who do not have the opportunity to leave. It will also undermine all I have said, for I have urged Christians not to desert our country in its time of need.' President Nyerere left on his own. Several weeks later this great Ethiopian pastor was strangled to death by government soldiers.

In the same country was a young man called Assefa who became a Christian in his early teens and led many high school students to faith. He was imprisoned on several occasions. On one occasion he heard some noise outside his prison cell, and was taken outside to see the bodies of two young men who had been shot dead. One of them had been led to Christ by Assefa. The soldiers said to Assefa, 'If you don't deny your faith, we will kill you too.' Assefa refused to deny his faith. For some reason known only to God the soldiers refrained from shooting him and several days later he was thrown out of the prison.

For years he had no home in which to live, and sometimes gathered his food from rubbish dumps. He was able to return to university only after the fall of the government. After graduating, he became General Secretary of the Ethiopian student movement, which throughout the 1990s drew in around a fifth of all university students in the country, with some 500 trained Bible study leaders. When they faced difficulties, people from Assefa's home village would say, 'You should go to the God of Assefa. He can deliver you.' Which of these two Ethiopian brothers showed the greater faith: the pastor who was strangled or Assefa? They both walked by faith, but the Lord saw fit to take one and to spare the other.

These illustrations could be multiplied many times. All showed great faith, whether in deliverance or in trials.

But then we are led to a further question. What motivated these Christian students, staff and graduates to stand firm and to live for Christ? I'd like to suggest three things.

1. They experienced the grace of God

The word 'grace' is unique to the New Testament, not found anywhere in other religious writing. It is used to describe the way in which God shows unmerited favour or sheer mercy. By grace God forgives our past sins and, as it were, forgets them. Several times in Scripture, God tells that after repentance he will 'remember our sins no more'.

I once explained this to a group of students in France. In the middle of the Bible study, a young girl cried out, 'Hallelujah!' I was surprised as she came from a traditional church background and was not used to expressive forms of faith. Several weeks later she sought me out privately.

'You know you've said God not only forgives but *forgets* our sins. Do you think that applies to all our sins?' she began.

'Yes', I replied. 'Why do you ask?'

Three years earlier she had had an abortion. She had been pressurized into doing so by her mother and she felt guilty. Could God forgive her for taking the life of an unborn child? I asked her to read the Scriptures again.

'Does God say, "I will remember your sins no more – except for abortion?" No, he says, "I will remember your sins no more." Full stop – no exceptions. You will of course have to live with the consequences of the loss of the child, but in eternal terms God has forgiven you and of his own volition has chosen to remember your sins no more.'

The 'forgetfulness of God' is a remarkable doctrine.

The 'forgetfulness of God' is a remarkable doctrine. It is a balm for all who are burdened by guilt. When we grasp this truth, we no longer find ourselves asking what *must* I do, but rather what *can* I do to serve such a wonderful God?

The wonder of God's grace was brought home to me again in a student conference in Argentina in 2001. There I met a Dutch missionary who had been involved in church planting in Irian Jaya after the Second World War, among people still living in Stone Age societies. He had seen thousands come to faith in a revival. He even saw reconciliation between those who had killed each other's family members before they were converted.

On the first night of the conference I spoke about the grace of

God. After the evening meeting I went out to enjoy the beautiful starlit night. He followed me. He thanked me, and then went on to say, 'Whenever I hear about the grace of God, it moves me deeply.' I asked him why. He told me that during the Second World War before he had become a Christian he had been a member of the Hitler Youth in Holland and had seen and done many terrible things. Yet despite this, God had drawn him to himself and, more, used him in revival in Irian Jaya.

'On one day I saw over two thousand people baptized,' he said. 'When I think of that, I am thankful for the sheer profundity of God's grace. Not only did he save me, but he used me like this despite my past.'

Beyond that, God shows his grace by strengthening us day by day in a way in which unbelievers know nothing; he gives the help and comfort of the Holy Spirit, the promises of Scripture and the encouragement of Christian brothers and sisters. Wang Ming Dao, one of the great preachers in the China Inter-Varsity Fellowship in the 1940s, was imprisoned for over thirty years, a good number of those spent in solitary confinement. The promises of Scripture kept him. When he was released in the 1980s a friend of mine interviewed him: 'You are now half blind and too weak to preach. Do you feel bitter that God allowed you to spend thirty years in prison?' Wang Ming Dao replied, 'No, for me my time in prison was a honeymoon with Jesus. I feel no bitterness.'

Why did he say that? Because he experienced the grace of God – in dealing with his past, in comforting him, in assuring him and in providing support for him in the midst of difficulty. We are able to bear the challenges of the call to sacrifice in student ministry because of the wonderful grace of God. In 2 Timothy 2, it is interesting that Paul reminds Timothy to be strong in the grace which is in Christ Jesus before he exhorts him to pass on the doctrines he has learnt and to endure hardship. A reminder of God's grace should always come before a call to sacrificial service – the grace of God is the motivation for sacrifice.

2. They were convinced of the truth of the gospel

In many parts of the world there can be an unhealthy emphasis on feelings and emotions. We should not deny the importance of the emotions as they are part of what makes us human. But the subjective must be governed, gripped and directed by objective convictions. Convictions need to revolve around our grasp of biblical truth.

I remember talking with some Chinese students in Portugal a few years ago. They had been invited by Portuguese students to their national conference. We were offering them New Testaments to take away to read for themselves. I asked one of them why he wanted to read the New Testament and I was intrigued by his thoughtful answer: 'The Portuguese Christian students are ordinary people just like us, and they have been very kind to us; so we have listened to what they believe because their faith is important to them. They have told us that Jesus is God who came in human form, and that the Bible is God's record of the work of Jesus. That is why we want to read it.'

It is only conviction of truth which will help students to stand firm for Christ.

I suggested to another that we meet together a few days later to discuss what he had read. When we met, I asked him what he thought of Jesus, as revealed in the Gospels. He told me he thought Jesus was very attractive, but it would be difficult for him to become a Christian because it might mean persecution when he returned home.

I said to him, 'The key question you need to answer for yourself is, "Do I think Jesus' claim to be the Saviour of the world is true?" If it is true, then you must follow him no matter what the consequences.' The next day we met again, and I asked if he had had time to reflect on this. He said, 'I believe Jesus is true and I want to follow him.' He knew it could be costly for him. He was convicted of the truth of the gospel. It is only conviction of truth which will help students to stand firm for Christ.

3. They looked forward to the hope of eternal life

One of the most powerful examples I have seen of this in recent years comes from Latin America. On 18 September 1997 on the outskirts of Quito, Ecuador, Neal Eldrenkamp, Media Secretary for IFES in Latin America, was shot dead by car thieves in front of his wife, Ruth, and young children, Jonathan and Luana. Jonathan was in Neal's arms when the car thieves shot and killed him. Two years later, at the same IFES World Assembly at which we heard from Grace Morillo, Ruth shared her testimony. After recalling her joint participation with Neal at previous World Assemblies, she said:

> Today I stand here alone. Jonathan, Luana and Natalia (born in November 1997) are back home in Buenos Aires and Neal is in our eternal home with our Lord. When he was shot to death almost two years ago, all our family dreams and ministry dreams were suddenly cut short. But why am I taking time to share these things with you?
>
> *First*, I need to thank you, my IFES family, for being a means of grace to my children and me. Your love, prayers, gifts and words of encouragement have meant we couldn't crash down even if we had chosen to. They have been sustaining as has been God's provision in my life through a God-fearing family, my church and the IFES movement.
>
> *Second*, I am here because I must witness to the kind of God we serve. Yes! He is the God of history, the sovereign Lord. Yet he has chosen to exercise his rule by giving his own Son and by taking upon himself the utmost pain of darkness and total separation and loss: consequences of our sin, so that we might live with him forever, and so that all creation may become what he intended it to be. He not only accompanies us in our suffering, but suffers on our behalf.

Third, I must remind myself and others this is the kind of world we live in – a broken world, full of emptiness, wrecked by injustice and consequent poverty and violence. The question then is not 'Why?' but 'Why not?' Why should we as Christians expect immunity from pain and loss while much of the world suffer them?

Last – and this is my main reason for speaking to you today – that brokenness is not the end of the story. Our pain is deep, but it is not all-encompassing; our loss is enormous, but it is not eternal; death is our enemy, but it does not have the final word. The wounded Lamb is also the Lion of Judah and one day he will reign in his perfect rule of love, peace and justice. Such is the hope of the gospel.

✢   ✢   ✢

Allow me to share a personal testimony at this point. In 1986, when I was working as European Regional Secretary in IFES, the Lord gave my wife and myself a beautiful daughter, Jessica Angharrad (which in Welsh means 'much loved'). Sadly she was born with an incurable illness, and died only a few months later. Because of the sustaining hope of the gospel, we wrote on her gravestone words which are similar to the words David uttered after God had seen fit to take his son. 'She cannot come to us, but we will go to her.' In doing so, we were echoing the same convictions of Ruth about her husband Neal. We look forward to the hope of eternal life, where we will be re-united with loved ones who have gone before us into the presence of Christ because they have loved him and followed him, and because of the sure and certain promise which he gave to his disciples: 'Where I go, you will be with me also.'

Why should we expect immunity from pain and loss while much of the world suffer them?

So it is that throughout the history of the church and the history of student ministry Christians have been prepared to sacrifice, because they tasted the grace of God, were convinced of the truth of the gospel, and looked forward to the hope of eternal life. The next generation can go on to repeat the great exploits of their forefathers if they live in the light of these three great truths.

9 : Providence and perseverance

My gift? ... I can persevere – I can plod in any given direction.
(William Carey)

Many have good beginnings, but few have good endings.
(Wang Ming Dao)

I find Caleb such an attractive character. At eighty-five years old
he says, 'I am still as strong today as the day Moses sent me out;
I'm just as vigorous to go out to battle now as I was then' (Joshua 14:11). He was referring back forty-five years to the time he and Joshua were sent as spies into the land of Israel. He still showed the courage, tenacity, zeal and perseverance of his early middle age – that is a rare quality. Many obstacles hinder the growth of a work of God and such a spirit of zealous perseverance and passion for his glory is wonderful to see. We will accomplish

> *I find Caleb such an attractive character.*

our task only through keeping our focus firmly on Christ and his purposes.

When he went to spy out the land, he was in a company of twelve. But ten reported back to headquarters that a military invasion was out of the question because the fortified cities were peopled with giants and the Israelites were only grasshoppers by comparison (Numbers 13:26–33). This was true, but Joshua and Caleb were not pessimistic. 'We should go up and take possession of the land, for we can certainly do it' (v. 30). His focus was not on the scale of the problem, but on God's capacity to intervene and bring blessing and victory. Thus God commended him: 'my servant Caleb has a different spirit and follows me wholeheartedly' (Numbers 14:24). God is looking for Calebs today.

It is always wonderful to see elderly Christians with a light in their eyes when they speak of their fixed determination to live for Christ. This resolve has characterized many great missionaries, and there has been no shortage of such fine people in the history of IFES.

Rate your stickability

Adoniram Judson – one of the first missionaries from North America
Adoniram Judson sensed God's call to serve overseas while a student at Yale. He was one of the founders of the Student Volunteer Movement, a forerunner of IFES, which was to send tens of thousands of missionaries. He and his wife Ann sailed from Massachusetts to India in 1812. Finding visa problems, they sailed on to Burma (now Myanmar), arriving in 1813. Judson's suffering is almost unparalleled in modern mission history.

He used time on his three-month voyage to study the issue of baptism, coming to a settled conviction that he and Ann should be baptized when they landed. Explaining this to supporters at home provoked a crisis. They cut all his financial support! This did start up again, but only after some very uncertain weeks.

It took over two years to grasp the rules of the Burmese language in a country where no English was spoken. It was six years before he saw the first Christian convert and in the rest of his lifetime he would see fewer than twenty-five, and perhaps only half that number had come to a living faith.

Adoniram Judson was suspected of being a spy during the war with Britain, and thrown into the 'Death Prison' (1824–1825) where he was hung upside down in leg irons every night.

Ann died in 1828 and this caused him to fall into a severe depression. For four months he sat by her grave, contemplating her decaying body and writing 'God to me is the great unknown; I believe in him but I cannot find him.' We can barely imagine such depths of bleakness for this man of God, so far from home. Added to this, several who initially professed faith fell away in the face of opposition.

Judson lost two wives and six children, and at least eleven co-workers. He died in obscurity. But one task was completed. The Burmese had the Bible in their own language.

In 1993, Paul Borthwick travelled to Myanmar for the 150th anniversary of Judson's translation of the Bible. In a meeting with youth leaders, he picked up a copy. The Burmese script was unintelligible to him, but he noticed an English sentence on the title page: 'Translated by Rev. A. Judson'. They still used the same translation now! What a testimony to Judson's scholarship and meticulous linguistic study, and what a legacy.

Paul was moved by this, and asked Matthew Hla Win, his host and translator, what he knew of Judson. Matthew replied, 'Whenever someone mentions Judson's name, tears come to my eyes because we know what he and his family suffered.' He went on with great emotion, 'Today there are six million Christians in Myanmar, and every one of us traces our spiritual heritage to one man – the Reverend Adoniram Judson.'

Was Judson a failure? In his lifetime he might have appeared so, but over the passage of history his work was vindicated by God. Too often we are ready to judge a ministry only in the short-term, but 'We will reap what we sow if we do not give up.'

One such is Francisco Mira Moya, General Secretary of the GBU in Spain. Francisco comes from Andalucía in Southern Spain. I recall speaking at a student leadership training event with him in Plencia on the Basque coast over Easter 1984. About forty students were there. Francisco was the only member of GBU staff, working part-time. The work was weak and existed in only a few towns around the country.

Under the regime of General Franco, Stacey Woods, the first General Secretary of IFES, wrote in 1964: 'Unless viewed from God's perspective, the idea of an evangelistic student movement in Spain is groundless optimism.' The work was begun soon afterwards by pioneers from Latin America. Samuel Escobar came to Madrid University on a year's sabbatical and started a weekly Bible study. Others continued it, including Ruth Siemens and several graduate students from Operation Mobilization like Stuart Park, a graduate of Cambridge University, and David Burt, a graduate of Oxford University. Jill Spink, also from Britain and a staff worker in London University, moved out to Salamanca in 1983 for a long period of service.

Perhaps the two most able students at that time were killed outright.

The Easter Conference in 1984 was my first visit to Spain as the new IFES Regional Secretary for Europe. Towards the end of the conference, a carload of students decided to drive into nearby Bilbao for an afternoon visit and possibly to buy a small gift for the visiting speaker. Tragically they were involved in a car accident and perhaps the two most able students in the national movement at that time were killed outright. Tuula Waris (twenty-four), the daughter of Finnish missionaries in northern Spain, was a medical student and led the group in Bilbao. Rolando González (nineteen), about to enter university, was the son of one of the pioneers of student work in Spain. Their brother and sister, Rodolfo González and Rayli Waris, were both badly injured. News reached the rest of the students at the camp. They were devastated. Until then levity and humour had characterized the conference. Suddenly the students were gripped by the reality of death and the seriousness and importance of the gospel. At the end of the conference many committed themselves to honour the testimony of these two young, zealous believers by seeking to strengthen the work of the gospel through the GBU in Spain.

Francisco and I went for a walk around the harbour at Plencia. I recall saying to him, 'Francisco, this movement is still weak. But the deaths of these two dear students has galvanized the other student leaders here. They need someone to give them direction and focus. Someone needs to give at least ten years to establish good foundations and to help the movement go on to make an impact for the gospel in the universities and in the broader society. It must be either you or Rodolfo.'

Francisco and his wife, Ana, determined that he should give the best years of his life to build the work of the gospel in the universities of Spain. As I write, he still serves as General Secretary over twenty years on. The movement is one of the most stable in Europe, staffed by keen and committed Spanish graduates and it has now spread to seventeen cities, with pioneering work in a further twelve cities all across the country. Altogether some 500 students are now in these groups. Francisco is greatly appreciated and respected throughout churches in Spain for the leadership, energy and commitment he has given. Through the sacrificial commitment of his staff team, we are seeing key church leaders formed whose influence is now beginning to spread throughout the country.

After losing two wonderfully able student leaders, it would have been easy to become dispirited and for Francisco to move on – but he persevered. His fine group of leaders include Rodolfo González who has served as Chairman or Vice-Chair of several national committees. Rodolfo is married to Jerka, who came from Yugoslavia, whom he met at an IFES international conference.

The mystery of God's providence

Student ministry in Bangladesh grew out of similar perseverance. Bob Cutler was a staff worker in the late 1960s and early 1970s with UCCF, the British student movement. Chua Wee Hian sought an experienced person to help set the direction of a student movement in Bangladesh and Bob's name was mentioned. On Wee Hian's invitation, Bob went out to Bangladesh in the mid 1970s. The country was emerging from great misery and suffering, including a nine-month war with Pakistan, before eventually gaining independence just a few years earlier in 1971. Millions had died or become refugees and the infrastructure needed to be rebuilt. Bob served there for over ten years, starting to pioneer groups in several cities, but his goal was to find an able Bangladeshi who could develop an indigenous ministry.

The Lord led him to a remarkable young man, Mihir Sarker. Bob invested in Mihir, spending time with him and his young family, and sending him off for three years' training at London Bible College. Mihir returned to Bangladesh in 1990, ready to take over from Bob after a year of working together. Just a few months after Bob returned to the UK in 1991, Mihir was travelling on a bus. The circumstances are not very clear but as he stepped down from the bus he was hit by another vehicle and killed instantly. The person in whom Bob had invested so much was suddenly taken to heaven. Bangladeshi students and graduates were devastated by the loss of their much-loved leader, as was the whole IFES family. Many felt Mihir would be a crucial leader for the church in Bangladesh, as well as a fine General Secretary for the student ministry. He was only thirty-seven years of age.

The Bangladeshi graduates could think of no better way forward than to invite Bob to return to Bangladesh to train another successor. But Bob was so exhausted that he had little inclination to return. However, though he did not understand the mysteries of God's providence, he remained committed to the cause of the gospel among university students in that country and agreed to serve for a further two years. When he returned, he gave time and energy to working alongside Peter Mazumder, a young graduate who had been a junior staff worker under Mihir. Peter still leads the work today, now with eight full-time staff.

The movement is gaining much respect. When Christian students in Dhaka University ran a workshop on 'Jesus Christ, Peacemaker' the departments of World Religion and of Peace & Conflict both supported it, and the Vice-Chancellor was happy to accept an invitation as chief guest. Some 500 students and faculty took away a copy of the New Testament or an evangelistic CD which the students and staff had produced.

The movement is gaining much respect.

There is now an established witness to Christ in nine universities, with a further five yet to be pioneered. The country suffers from frequent cyclones and flooding, and able graduates could be tempted to emigrate. We thank God for the staff working on low salaries, who persist in their commitment to students. That commitment extends beyond its borders and the Bangladeshi staff are helping to pioneer an IFES movement in one of the tough remaining countries with no witness to Christ on its campuses.

Liberia

I have often been left in wonder at God's preservation of his servants during war and civil turmoil. When the war broke out in Monrovia, the capital of Liberia, between rebel forces and the government in 1996, John Buseh (General Secretary of the Liberian Student Movement), the staff and fifty student leaders were at an Easter training camp. By the end of the camp they were trapped. After two days their supplies ran out. They were surrounded by rebel soldiers. John tried to approach the rebels but was scared stiff as people were usually killed indiscriminately.

These rebels had a reputation of rape and of forcing people to march with them as they moved on from county to county, town to town and village to village. They threatened to rape the women students at the camp. The men made a human wall around the women and they prayed to the Lord all night. Miraculously the women were not harmed.

Next day they walked thirty-five kilometres, their few belongings on their heads, to Monrovia, a 'safe zone' at that time. They met a group of fully armed rebel fighters on the way, who demanded money and anything of value along with shoes and watches. They all arrived safely, though some students found their homes looted and burnt down.

During the second phase of the armed conflict (2000–04) LIFES students formed groups to reach rural communities with the gospel, providing basic care and amenities despite the difficulties and the threats of war. Regardless of the cost and the dangers, they often trekked long distances to carry out these evangelistic campaigns.

A miraculous provision of fish

In the same way, God was pleased to answer the prayers of a group of students in North Africa in the early 1990s. In this Muslim majority country, the church numbered only a few hundred.

Many students from sub-Saharan French-speaking Africa go there on government scholarships to enhance their education. Among those who arrived one year were several Christians who had been active in student movements in their own countries. Naturally, they looked for fellowship with other believers, and started Bible study groups. These began in just one or two cities, but spread to over ten locations. Soon the leaders were planning their first national conference. They were poverty-stricken, but in faith booked a campsite on the Mediterranean coast for a leadership training event. Twenty-seven gathered together. They had spent all their money paying for the campsite and had no money left over to buy food!

They had a guitar with them, so they went down to the beach on the first evening and began to sing some songs of praise to the Saviour as the sun set and twilight descended. While they were singing, a fishing boat approached, perhaps attracted by their music. The fishermen jumped out of the boat and walked up to find out what they were doing. Despite language difficulties, they managed to explain that they were singing Christian songs. They told the fishermen openly that they wanted to reach out to students in the universities of this Muslim majority country. They also shared their unfortunate position of not having enough money to buy food. The sailors explained that they too were believers – Korean fishermen far away from home. 'We've caught lots of fish today. You can share our catch.' The African students were delighted! Hardly the feeding of the 5,000, but maybe we can call it the feeding of the twenty-seven! The Korean Christian fishermen returned each day for the rest of the week and brought fresh fish to feed the young African students. This was surely God's hand of providence. He had honoured their persevering pioneering spirit.

Chris Davies: perseverance and vision

There are evangelical publishing houses now in eight countries in Eastern Europe. Chris Davies, a staff worker with the British movement until the late 1970s, had the eye of faith to see that communism would collapse and that many new Christians in the Eastern Bloc would then need help to grow into maturity. She travelled to Hungary four times a year into the 1980s, working to support and strengthen Christian students. It was a secret work known to hardly anyone in the West, often lonely and needing solid and prayerful determination. Chris loved to train students in how to lead group Bible studies and in how to use the Gospel records in evangelism. With great care she and a handful of evangelicals within Hungary ran small student camps and slowly the work built up. It is now one of the strongest movements in Europe with groups in university towns across the country – and in 2004 it hosted our major European students' conference on evangelism.

In 1985 Chris talked with me about the need to mobilize ourselves for Christian publishing so we would be ready to translate and commission books as soon as this could move forward. She had evidently sensed a prompting of the Holy Spirit, and our conversation led to the founding of the East European Literature Advisory Committee (EELAC), a joint venture between IFES and OM. Its aim was 'to cultivate national authors and to produce books of enduring worth'. We now have over 850 titles published in fifteen languages. The publishing house in Hungary has seen remarkable growth, both in its range of titles and in its nurturing of Hungarian authors. Kornél Herjeczki, a leading haematologist in Budapest, now

It was a secret work known to hardly anyone in the West.

gives most of his time to directing it. He was one of the students Chris Davies met in her quiet visits and he caught her vision and shares the same persevering spirit.[1]

Chris died in 1992, aged forty-four. She had a fragile temperament and a gentle and vulnerable spirit; over the years at times she suffered from depression. She persevered and her life was an eloquent testimony to what Christ can do through us if we are willing.

How IVP was born

Chris Davies showed a characteristic that lies behind all our major initiatives and which we have already seen in this book. She looked at what was and she saw what could be. 'Dissatisfaction' is not listed in the New Testament *charisma*, yet Paul's teaching is steeped in it. He continually expresses a deep desire for more – for more of Christ in his own experience; for more of Christ in the churches he had planted; for more of Christ in the lives of each believer. We read of his daily concern for the churches and we hear the longing in his prayers for Christians to gain an ever-deeper understanding of their inheritance in Christ. All staff who want to influence students and to stretch their aspirations show this continual desire for more and for better.

The first evangelical publishing house set up by an IFES movement was Inter-Varsity Press in the UK. The IVP imprints in the UK and the USA have commanded wide respect and their books have gone into over sixty languages. Including the work in Eastern Europe they now have sister publishers in over thirty nations, serving much of the world. Each is rooted in the IFES movement in that country. So today, students, graduates and the church more widely have access to commentaries, doctrine and a wide range of books for Christians in the professions, helping them grapple with issues in a robust and biblical manner. But this was not always so. Here is how the story began:

When the British Inter-Varsity Fellowship (IVF) was founded, the few Christian books available at the time were rather pietistic, with little to engage the mind as well as the heart. The small IVF staff under Douglas Johnson (always known as 'DJ') felt a keen sense of dissatisfaction about this on behalf of their students. So DJ recruited a young Birmingham University graduate, Ronald Inchley, to help him address this. Ronald Inchley (always known as 'RI') was a self-taught musician and gifted actor and the first of his family ever to go to university. Recalling RI's influence in Birmingham University Christian Union, DJ invited him to 'assist in the production of literature'. Up to that time the Fellowship had produced just three stapled booklets and the story of the still-emerging IVF – written by a young Donald Coggan, later to become Archbishop of Canterbury.

RI was a perceptive man with a sharp instinct. He persevered in that same spirit, wanting more and better for students and graduates. For the next thirty years he was frequently seen in student conferences listening hard to discussions, engaging students over meals and making careful notes. He wanted books to speak right into their situations. He got to know many of the writers he would later publish while they were students. He recognized their gifts and could see how their skills were already being honed. In short, he glimpsed how God could use them as they matured.

He had established a publishing house which merited the attention of the nation.

When RI died in 2005, major UK newspapers carried obituaries for him. He had established a publishing house which was to have worldwide influence in his lifetime – it merited the attention of the nation, not just of the church.[2]

Pressing on

What can we learn from the lives of persevering saints?

1. *God has his own timetable.* As Eugene Petersen puts it, 'Discipleship is a long obedience in the same direction.' We are often governed by a desire for a quick fix. Samuel Escobar remarked shrewdly that the only thing discovered in the twentieth century was speed. God has his own timetable and sometimes grows a work more slowly than we would wish. As Scripture says, 'We shall reap if we faint not.'

2. *We must believe in the promises of God.* When you hit tough times, remember God's promises and hold fast to them. Hebrews 10:35–36 says 'So do not throw away your confidence; it will be richly rewarded. You need to persevere so that when you have done the will of God, you will receive what he has promised.'

3. *It is good to keep a sense of perspective.* When we feel ready to give up, the enemy can hit us with a sense of isolation, like he did Elijah (1 Kings 19). God had to remind him that he had several thousand servants still in Israel. It is easy to feel we are the only ones going through a particular experience. We need to remember that others are going through the same thing and that the Lord Jesus has also run this race.

4. *We should maintain a thankful spirit.* Every major challenge is an opportunity for growth. No-one ever achieved godly character through the laying on of hands. Charisma may come in an instant, but character takes a lifetime. As Peter Kuzmic from Croatia has said, 'Charisma without character spells catastrophe!' When we are under pressure, when our dreams and visions seem to have died, when everything seems almost too hard to bear, this is the season that forms character. So be positive and look to God with a spirit of thankfulness. As Scripture says, we are called to 'give thanks in everything', or in the midst of all situations.

5. *We can know God as Father.* When I first read John Calvin's *Institutes of the Christian Religion*, I wrote to Hugh Goddard, an IFES worker then pioneering student ministry in Lebanon. I explained that I had discovered I was a slave, a *doulos*, of Christ. He quickly wrote back to me to say 'If that's all you are, you are no different from a Muslim. You are not just a slave, you are a *son*.' He was right. This assurance of being sons and daughters of the living God gives us an urgent desire to press on and to bring him glory and honour.

6. *We must work to finish well.* In everything God gives us, there is a finishing line. Jesus was given work to do by his father and he knew he was going to be able to say 'It is finished'. For all of us, in every vocation, there is a finishing line, a moment when we too can say the task is completed. We must make every effort to keep running until we have fulfilled God's calling to us in that vocation – until we have completed the task, or handed the baton to someone else who can go on to complete the task.

7. *Some sow, some plant, some reap.* Our task may be to sow, with others carrying on from where we leave off. I remember a cross-cultural worker in Iran saying, 'I've served for forty years and seen very little fruit. I don't think I have even done much planting, but I have cleared away a lot of rubble so someone else can come in and build.' That shows God's sense of timing, an awareness of one's own small contribution, and a resolve to lay the groundwork for others.

10 : Looking ahead

The harvest is plentiful but the workers are few. Ask the Lord of the harvest, therefore, to send out workers into his harvest field.
(Matthew 9:37–38)

He thanked me for this noble vision, centred on God's word and discipleship. He sensed it had prophetic implications.
(pioneering in Equatorial Guinea)

We move to a close with a critical question: How can IFES movements best serve Christ's church around the world? This will always be the pivotal question to ask. I quoted Bobby Sng from Singapore in Chapter 5 when we looked at students' contribution to society. He was right to suggest that our investment in their lives is best judged twenty years later. That is when we see a maturing fruit of our labour under God.

How can IFES movements best serve Christ's church around the world?

My hope and prayer is that students, staff and supporters will keep bright the vision God has given us. To do that we must teach each generation where we have come from and how the Lord has helped us on the way. Some of the lessons learned and principles forged have been at great cost. So as we look ahead we remind ourselves again of Martin Luther's warning, quoted at the beginning of Chapter 1, that there is nothing so short as a Christian's memory, and of the repeated exhortation to the Israelites to 'remember'.

At the International Conference of Evangelical Students held in Cambridge in 1939, the students and graduates sang a hymn often to be sung in conferences afterwards, anchoring their trust in God:

We rest on thee, our shield and our defender
We go not forth alone against the foe
Strong in thy strength, safe in thy keeping tender
We rest on thee, and in thy name we go.

War broke out within a few months of that conference and IFES was not formally founded until 1947. Yet the commitment to one another was firmly established.

The apostle Paul did not hold back in asking for prayer, and I echo his plea in asking your prayer for the student world. You have read of many needs already. In these closing pages you will read more of our desire to finish the task of pioneering new movements and of challenges ahead in the Muslim world. May the Lord help us to be very courageous in our sowing, planting, watering and building in students' lives, for many of them have shown extraordinary courage. I ask your prayer for three key areas.

1. China

In 1948 the British Inter-Varsity Fellowship made an ambitious silent movie called *The Decisive Years*, bringing to the Christian public the needs and opportunities of student ministry through-out the world. It ranged first around the UK and Ireland, then North America before panning across the continents, showing countries where IFES was already established and the sheer magnitude of the task ahead. In one poignant frame the following words appear:

CHINA

Christian students in China are destined to witness in difficult days

It was prophetic. On 1 October 1949 Chairman Mao declared in Peking's Tiananmen Square that the people of China had 'stood up' and in 1950 the student movement in China, the largest founding member of IFES, closed down. Through the previous twenty years, God in his grace had been preparing leaders for the church whose news would be virtually lost to the world for the next twenty years.

Here was a new generation of student evangelists.

I recall a report in the UK Christian press of the student demonstration in Tiananmen Square in 1989. OMF's China Researcher Tony Lambert was there and found himself listening almost in disbelief to the strains of hymn singing. The first open-air service for forty years! Students courageously declared their faith to their communist government and to the world's media. The church in China may have been driven underground but it could not die, and here was a new generation of student evangelists to prove it.

As Tony Lambert talked with students there, he found that a group of them had discovered the writings of Francis Schaeffer. They were excited by this as they had been hoping to find the principles behind democracy and freedom. Through Schaeffer's writings they were led straight to the Bible.

We have no formal movement in China now, but we thank God for all he is doing among its millions of students.[1] The Chinese house church movement is spreading from the country into cities and largely through it we are witnessing the re-emergence of a great work of God among students. As groups are not allowed to meet on campus, the house church leaders are actively developing coordinated ministry strategies, and dozens of student groups are meeting with links to this network, some with over 100 members. A friend of the Fellowship writes:

> Painfully aware of the spiritual vacuum generated by atheistic ideology, and severely wounded and frustrated by political and social distortion, students are seeking answers and yearning for healing. The gospel finds large numbers of open-hearted listeners in the university community and is drawing many into new life in Christ.
>
> Besides students, university faculty members are also being converted. Many take leadership roles in the student groups, and some are becoming active in social and political engagement.

China's influence on the world is set to be unrivalled. The Beijing Olympics, entry into the World Trade Organization, and the now massive tide of students and graduates travelling eastwards and westwards all give hope for further radical change over the next ten years.

2. The Muslim world

We do not publish a list of countries where we are still working to establish an evangelical student movement, but, as this book goes to press, they number eighteen, including some of the toughest Islamic and totalitarian states in the world.

As movements have been born, and national leadership set in place in more and more nations, we have given God the glory.

Bringing the gospel to Muslim students

We have unprecedented opportunity to bring the gospel to Muslim students. But what comes to mind first when we think of Islam? Perhaps terrorism, oil wealth, the burka or the call to prayer. Misunderstandings and lack of awareness have bred several myths about Christian mission to the 1.1 billion followers of Islam. There are undeniable challenges for us, but lack of information can distort the true picture.

- *Myth 1: The Muslim world is uniformly hostile to the gospel.* Christian ministry is difficult in the Gulf States, but there is increasing openness in some nominally Islamic nations, including the Central Asian Republics of the former Soviet Union. Some of these peoples know little Islamic doctrine except for practices embedded in their culture, such as circumcision or burial ceremonies. (See *Operation World* for more details.[2])
- *Myth 2: The Islamic world is dominated by North Africa and the Middle East.* What has become known as the 10:40 Window still forms the heartland of Islamic fundamentalism, but large numbers of Muslims are to be found elsewhere. While Asia holds the greatest number, Islam is also growing in sub-Saharan Africa. The highest number of Muslims in one nation is in Indonesia.
- *Myth 3: It is impossible to witness in countries under* Sharia law. In one country under *Sharia* law, ministry has begun among several hundred students. Our God moves despite political restrictions. Nothing is impossible for him. The governance of nations with significant populations of Muslim and Christian peoples will always be extremely sensitive. When we hear news of unrest in countries such as Nigeria or Sudan, where the countries are equally divided between these faith groupings, we sense something of the depth of tension. We have seen students show wonderful courage in sharing their faith. Staff and Christian leaders need to model well how to do this wisely.

- *Myth 4: Muslims are unable to hear the gospel in Islamic nations.* There are at least four key ways in which the gospel is being shared with Muslims. *First*, every country in the world is now covered by Christian radio and TV transmissions. Initiatives like SAT-7 have sent thousands of Christian programmes into the Muslim world.[3] Muslims can tune in to Christian truth in their own language. *Second*, many Christians take their professions into the Islamic world to bring the presence of Christ into those nations. *Third*, students from Islamic countries come to the West to study. One North African, himself converted from Islam while studying in Europe, is working with students in a major European city. He holds regular debates with Islamic mullahs and students on subjects such as 'God's forgiveness in the Koran and the Bible' and 'Jesus Christ, Prophet of Islam?' These can draw 100 students at any one time. *Fourth*, students can hear the gospel through Christian Arabs. There are now Christian student fellowships in universities in many parts of North Africa and the Middle East.
- *Myth 5: Egypt and Sudan are gateways for Islam.* Egypt and the Sudan have often been viewed as gateways for Islam into Africa. But Christian students view these countries differently. Could they be the gateway for the gospel into the Gulf? In both these countries there is a vibrancy about the students' witness and a deep desire to see Christ's name glorified.

3. Unpioneered countries and universities

What is it like to pioneer a new movement? In some places it has taken many years; in others the initial work has been much quicker. In April 2005, Gideon Para-Mallam from Nigeria made his first visit to our 150th country, Equatorial Guinea, which is bordered by Cameroon and Gabon. *Special Report* magazine gave a glimpse of that exciting week.[4]

Diary of a pioneer

Monday 11 April 2005. A year of waiting and praying. Today I began daily visits to the Embassy in Lagos, coming up against all kinds of arbitrary conditions.

Friday 14 April. Almost gave up, but got a surprise call from a lady I had not met, urging me on, saying the trip would be worth it.

Monday 18 April. At 11am I handed in the final document. They then asked for *another* letter from the IFES International Office. I was dismayed. An elderly woman interpreter urged me in English, 'My country needs you; my people are under bondage. I really want you to get this visa.' I was touched by her plea in front of other Embassy staff. I called the office in Oxford, UK and Kirsty Thorburn responded swiftly. I had it within half an hour. The visa was offered around 3.15pm; the last plane departed at 4.45pm. Lagos traffic was building up, but to God's glory I made it by just five minutes.

Tuesday 19 April. Landed in Malabo. Most passengers had cases ransacked and money demanded by the young Customs lady. I escaped, but then two security guards in plain clothes collected my passport and that of a Nigerian pastor, demanding money. We refused. A pastor from Malabo intervened, but the guards just tucked the passports away from view. We stood there helpless. The Guinean Pastor had to pay before we had them returned. My spirit was wounded and very low. I knew things could be tough but hardly expected this. The urgency in my heart grew – we needed a vibrant evangelical student movement which could make a difference. Accommodation is sparse and the hotels expensive. I found a Red Cross facility with a bed, water in buckets, and no more.

Wednesday 20 April. Met with an elderly Christian businessman who was the country's first Ambassador to Nigeria. He was cautiously helpful. The Universidad Nacional De Guinea Ecuatorial is the only university, with campuses in Malabo and Bata. Made my way to Malabo campus, sharing a taxi with a young Guinean who spoke some English. He asked if I was a professor. I said I taught students the Bible. Just like the Ethiopian and Philip, he said he'd been looking for someone to teach him the Bible. Adolfos gave his life to Jesus after I explained the gospel, and became my first interpreter.

Thursday 21 April. To Bata. Met by the Nigerian Consul-General, and stayed with him two nights. The Consulate Interpreter – also a pastor – came with me to the campus. Three students want to be part of an IFES group. We talked with a Ghanaian pastor who was deeply touched when he realized IFES was a grassroots movement. For seven years he had ministered to foreign English-speaking Christians, and longed to draw in the Guineans. 'IFES seems to get it right from the start', he said. I was elated and left some copies of *Praise and Prayer*.

Saturday 23 April. Back to Malabo. The first student I met was joined by three others. With a local pastor as interpreter I shared the vision of IFES: discipleship, evangelism, missions and leadership development. I told stories from around the IFES world. After their questions, I asked the students if they would spearhead a movement. 'Yes!' they said. (It won't be easy. Lectures are in shifts from 8am–1pm and 2pm–8pm. Any meeting of more than five students needs special permission – usually denied.) Fruitful meeting with church leaders. The Vice-President thanked me for 'this noble vision, centred on God's word and discipleship'. He said it would breathe fresh air into the country's students and sensed it had 'prophetic implications'.

In October that year Gideon returned to find the pastors had gathered over fifty students from different campuses to meet with him. At that meeting the Equatorial Guinea Evangelical Student Association (EGESA) was formally launched with a group of chosen leaders and senior advisers. Four months later it sent its own representative to the IFES West Africa Consultation on HIV / AIDS held in Lagos. So this brand new fellowship is now being grafted into the IFES family.

This brand new fellowship is now grafted into the IFES family.

The threats may be different for each culture and context, but they will always be real, for the university is the seat of human influence.

I close with Paul's exhortation to the Philippian Christians, which we adopt as our own to students on every continent:

> Whatever happens, conduct yourselves in a manner worthy of the gospel of Christ. Then, whether I come and see you or only hear about you in my absence, I will know that you stand firm in one spirit, contending as one man for the faith of the gospel without being frightened in any way by those who oppose you (Philippians 1:27–28).

Students need our prayers as they proclaim and defend the truth of the gospel at the cutting edge of their generation and of their culture.

There is still much work to do. In the countries where student ministry has begun, many campuses still need to be pioneered and each generation has the responsibility to reach their peer group. May you, as you read this book, discern which part you can play, and may the Lord help you to fulfil your calling for his kingdom with all the gifts which he has placed at your disposal.

Appendix 1 : What *distinctive* contribution has IFES brought to the global church?

Our five-fold contribution

1. *Equipping generations of students and graduates to love doctrine*

We urge students and graduates not only to believe the gospel but to learn to articulate, defend, and contend for it. This robustness can be lost in much contemporary evangelicalism.

We work to model the apostle Paul's pattern of rooting young Christians in doctrine as a basis for how to live.

Nurturing a love of doctrine has been a central plank of the movement from the start. The first-ever IVP book was T. C. Hammond's *In Understanding be Men*.[1] Closely linked is our training of student leaders to think from principle. *Student Witness and Christian Truth* by Bob Horn (later General Secretary of UCCF) made a seminal contribution here, becoming one of the most talked-about books of its generation; his *From Cambridge to the World*, co-authored with Oliver Barclay, uses the history of the Cambridge Inter-Collegiate Christian Union (CICCU) to illustrate the same ground for students now.

When I became General Secretary, John Stott wrote to me quoting the words of John Newton: 'Lindsay, I hope you will be like iron in the essentials and a reed in the non-essentials.' This distinction is critical for the student leaders and staff of our national movements. We must be unwavering on the central truths of the gospel and able to distinguish them from denominational practice. (See Appendix 2.)

2. Thoughtful, persuasive and creative evangelism

We seek to train students in contentful, persuasive and creative evangelism, equipping them to answer honest questions robustly, and to present the gospel in a thoughtful and attractive way that captures the imagination of fellow students. It may be through Gospel distribution, personal testimony, public proclamation or apologetics, together with music or drama. Students bring passion, energy and imagination to this. We nurture skills in apologetic evangelism, as our gospel is reasonable and defensible and we believe the Holy Spirit will lead us into all truth.

We urge students to ask questions they may not be asking. In the 'i-generation' where trivial information crowds out the major issues, where experience is king, and where all is seen as relative, we still work to evoke questions of *truth*. We owe it to students to help them into timeless issues which the spirit of the age obliterates.

3. Discipleship or Formación

We work to nurture Christian students in Bible study and prayer. We encourage them: (i) to relate their faith to their personal lives and to their academic work; and (ii) to recognize the ethical implications of the gospel in the public arena. A major contribution of IFES has been a focus on the Christian mind, not least through book publishing.

4. Leadership and expansion of the church globally

We work to provide the church with pastors and leaders who love truth and are committed to the authority of Scripture.

We work to build a grasp of world mission as part of the character of God through teaching programmes and major conferences.

We encourage students to participate in mission exposure trips and thousands become cross-cultural career missionaries.

In each country the IFES movement works among overseas students as well as nationals.

IFES was in the vanguard of mobilizing Christians in the non-Western world for mission. Students and graduates from some of the poorest nations pioneered student ministry cross-culturally from the late 1940s. It took over twenty years for this to be an accepted model of mission.

5. Christian publishing to strengthen the church globally
The Inter-Varsity Press (IVP) grew out of the British movement and now has sister publishing houses in over thirty nations, serving much of the world. In the 1974 Lausanne Congress, Ian Rennie, a Canadian historian of Scottish descent, said, 'IVP has been one of the most crucial factors in the renaissance of evangelical theology globally since the Second World War.' Each publishing house produces evangelistic books, doctrinal books, Bible commentaries and apologetics, all consonant with the IFES doctrinal basis. We work to illustrate biblical truth for each generation and context, and to nurture new indigenous authors. In an age where students turn more instinctively to cyberspace than to the printed word, we remain committed to instilling a love for books, and to producing books of enduring worth.

Appendix 2 : What we believe

All IFES national movements unite around these central truths of Christianity, as revealed in Scripture:

1. The unity of the Father, Son and Holy Spirit in the Godhead.
2. The sovereignty of God in creation, revelation, redemption and final judgment.
3. The divine inspiration and entire trustworthiness of Holy Scripture, as originally given, and its supreme authority in all matters of faith and conduct.
4. The universal sinfulness and guilt of all men since the fall, rendering them subject to God's wrath and condemnation.
5. Redemption from the guilt, penalty, dominion and pollution of sin, solely through the sacrificial death (as our Representative and Substitute) of the Lord Jesus Christ, the incarnate Son of God.
6. The bodily resurrection of the Lord Jesus Christ from the dead and his ascension to the right hand of God the Father.
7. The presence and power of the Holy Spirit in the work of regeneration.

8. The justification of the sinner by the grace of God through faith alone.
9. The indwelling and work of the Holy Spirit in the believer.
10. The one Holy Universal Church which is the Body of Christ and to which all true believers belong.
11. The expectation of the personal return of the Lord Jesus Christ.

Why do we have a doctrinal basis?

In 1 Timothy 4:16 Paul exhorts Timothy to 'Watch your life and doctrine closely. Persevere in them, because if you do, you will save both yourself and your hearers.'
In 1 Timothy 4:13–15 he warns against many people being swayed by false teaching and urges:

> Devote yourself to the public reading of Scripture, to preaching and to teaching. Do not neglect your gift, which was given you through a prophetic message when the body of elders laid their hands on you.
>
> Be diligent in these matters; give yourself wholly to them, so that everyone may see your progress.

Our doctrinal basis is our anchor 'to keep us from being wrecked on the rocks of error or stranded on the shoals of spiritual ineffectiveness'. (Stacey Woods, IFES founding General Secretary)

Doctrine is central to the biblical message
Doctrine is mentioned no fewer than fifty times in the New Testament. When we speak of it, we are talking about God's truth. Note Paul's exhortations in 2 Timothy to:

- *retain* the standard of sound words that you have heard (1:13)
- *guard* the treasure which has been entrusted to you (1:14)

- *entrust* to faithful men the things you have heard from me (2:2)
- *preach* the word ... for the time will come when they will not endure sound doctrine (4:3)

We can learn from past mistakes

The Student Volunteer Movement (SVM) had a powerful impact on the missionary vision of the student world and the wider church for sixty years, as we saw in Chapter 1. But it lost its way, drifting into ecumenism. It became committed to visible unity with professing Christians from a variety of church backgrounds without a formal summary of Christian doctrine at its centre. It never had an agreed doctrinal basis. Similarly the Student Christian Movement, from which the founding members of the British Inter-Varsity Fellowship seceded, drifted from its original passion for Christ. These movements lost their way evangelistically because they lost their roots doctrinally.

From the start IFES leaders emphasized that we are not ecumenical, but evangelical, for we are people of the evangel, of the gospel. Under the guidance of Martyn Lloyd-Jones, the first Executive Committee drew up a summary of key biblical truths to keep us focusing on central matters and to save us from majoring on minors.

Reasons for teaching doctrine

Scripture gives several reasons why it is important to teach doctrine. Here are three:

- *Refreshment*. In the Song of Moses (Deuteronomy 32:1–2) God says his doctrine will come like the dew of the morning which refreshes the grass, or like the rain on the grass. Doctrine refreshes the life of the Christian. It provides a balanced diet of the great truths of Scripture which, if taught well, will create healthy individual Christians and healthy campus groups.

- *Unity.* It will provide the foundation for unity, not act as a source of division (1 Corinthians 3:9–11). Biblical truth pulls us together as individuals and as a body (hence 'the belt of truth' in Ephesians 6:14). Robin Wells, formerly a member of the IFES Executive Committee and General Secretary of UCCF, used to describe the doctrinal basis as both 'a minimum and a maximum' statement of faith. It includes all the primary truths of the gospel, while omitting – and therefore giving liberty on – matters of secondary importance like forms of church governance, infant or adult baptism or the practice of gifts. To require a particular stance in these areas would go beyond Scripture. So we teach students to unite around the primaries and let the secondaries remain secondary, hence the name 'Christian Union' by which campus groups are often known.
- *Freedom and stability.* The Lord Jesus taught that grasping biblical truth leads to liberation. In John 8:32 we read: 'Then you will know the truth, and the truth will set you free.' It also provides stability as learning more of God's character and his work in the world and in eternity deepens our understanding of his concern for us.

Through main teaching programmes and through small groups, we work to articulate these key truths so they fill students with a sense of wonder at the glory of the gospel. For that alone will give them passion and drive to explain and proclaim it to their classmates, and in due course to their family and in the workplace, and on to the ends of the earth. That is what we are all about!

We pray God will keep giving us staff and board members who love truth and have a desire and commitment to teach it clearly in a student context. Where people show indifference to doctrine, or lack of passion for it, they have generally not grasped the beauty of truth revealed to us: truth about our triune God, and about his purposes for us and for the world.

Appendix 3 : How to pray for students [1]

Paul prayed with longing and joy for the churches he served – would you pray for Christian students in the same way?

The world's universities are influential places, where ideas and philosophies are born and grow. Students today will be the future decision-makers in every field – education, science and technology, law, commerce, the media.

The Lord Jesus Christ is the one in whom are hidden all treasures of wisdom and knowledge. Yet any concept of truth is now largely discounted and the Lord's name ignored or held in dishonour. Christian students have to cope with insidious and often strong opposition to their faith.

Universities in some countries are huge, with a fifth of a million students. Most universities have several thousand students; many colleges are only a fraction of that size.

They each reflect the situation in their country. For example:

- In turbulent times universities are closed.
- After war or genocide students struggle with the trauma of personal loss and of what they saw and heard.

- In affluent countries students tend to be less serious about study.
- In totalitarian regimes there are typically no meeting places for students outside class time.
- In countries afflicted by HIV/AIDS, tens of thousands of students are affected.

Believe what you like?

Are students free to believe what they like? That's not a simple question. There is great pressure in Islamic, Buddhist and Hindu nations to observe the faith of the land. In communist countries, Christian meetings are not allowed on campus. It takes real courage to be a Christian in these situations, and sometimes Christians have to remain secret believers. In the West the insidious pressures of materialism and pleasure-seeking squeeze out any sense of the need for salvation. But our sovereign God can break into students' hearts.

Athens then and now

The apostle Paul gave a forthright address to the intellectuals in Athens (Acts 17), presenting to them the God who is not far from any of us and who wants us to 'reach out for him and find him'. When the Athenians heard about the resurrection some sneered, others said they would like to hear more – and a few believed. We see the same reactions today.

A strong student ministry feeds a strong national church.

Often students fear the gospel would limit their freedom. They know it has moral implications and sometimes these seem just too great. We must pray for the Holy Spirit to convince students of their need of a Saviour and of what it means to be truly free.

Year after year we see thousands profess faith around the world. For some it is the reasoned argument of the speaker that matters. For others, in a society of fractured relationships, it is the emphasis on a God who wants us to know him personally.

Praying for staff

Paul, the itinerant missionary, asked prayer for:

- boldness (Ephesians 6:19–20)
- opportunity and clarity (Colossians 4:3–4)
- protection (2 Thessalonians 3:2–3)

Would you pray these things for the staff? Pray too for their families, some with young children. Staff often have to travel long distances and be away frequently from their home and their church.

Praying for students

A guide for daily prayer

Sunday – SPIRITUAL LIVES
Discipline of personal Bible study and prayer often starts in student days. Pray for: (a) a desire to understand Scripture, to love it and to let it shape behaviour; (b) strong links with a local church in term-time and at home; (c) fellowship with other Christians where there is no church; (d) a desire to read, and books of enduring worth for students and graduates.

Monday – ACADEMIC STUDY
Focusing on study can be hard for students who have to work part-time to pay their fees; and for overseas students who struggle with

the language. Pray that Christians will: (a) prioritize their work; (b) develop a biblical world-view. Ask the Lord for graduates who will shake salt and shine light in their field of expertise.

Tuesday – EVANGELISM
The student world gives wonderful opportunities for evangelism. Pray for: (a) Christian students to have clarity on the truth of the gospel – and a willingness both to defend it and to declare it; (b) God to work in the hearts of unbelievers; (c) appropriate methods of evangelism; (d) freedom where governments do not allow students to share their faith openly.

Wednesday – WORLD MISSION
Thousands of serving missionaries sensed their call to mission while they were students. Pray for: (a) a grasp of the missional heart of God; (b) friendships with international students; (c) student mission conferences held regularly around the world; (d) graduating students to consider serving in spiritual ministry, either cross-culturally or within their culture.

Thursday – LEADERSHIP
New leaders are needed every year, at every level. Some students lead groups which are bigger than the average church. Leaders of Bible studies or prayer meetings can help shape members' lives as much as those who serve on committees. Pray leaders will 'keep watch over [themselves] and all the flock' (Acts 20:28). Paul saw the danger of leaders neglecting their own spiritual lives.

Friday – PIONEERING
There are still countries with a university system but no IFES movement. Pray for a movement to begin in these places and for God to give us national students with leadership skills who may, in his time, become staff, so an indigenous work can be established.

Saturday – FAMILIES AND FRIENDSHIP

Many students come from broken homes, or from homes alien to the gospel. Family relationships have a bearing on our whole lives. Pray for reconciliation where that is needed. Sexual purity is always under threat. Pray students will find older friends – perhaps in church – with whom they can talk when they need to. Pray that new Christians will know God's grace in all areas of life and find strong and wholesome friendships.

We publish regular bulletins for prayer, in print and by email. To receive them, please go to www.ifesworld.org/pray

Appendix 4 : IFES national movements

Founding members in 1947

Australia
Canada
China
France
Great Britain
Netherlands
New Zealand
Norway
Switzerland
USA

IFES-linked ministry now[1]

Movements in several countries are not affiliated formally to the worldwide Fellowship for reasons of political sensitivity. In some countries the movement is still working towards affiliation. This process can take several years while a national board is established and, where possible, relationships are built with national church leaders. Whether a movement is affiliated to IFES or works in close fellowship with us, we serve them in the same way.

English and Portuguese-speaking Africa

Angola	GBECA	Grupos Bíblicos de Estudantes Cristãos de Angola
Botswana	ICCM	Inter-College Christian Movement of Botswana
Eritrea		
Ethiopia	EvaSUE	Evangelical Students Union of Ethiopia
Equatorial Guinea	EGESA	Equatorial Guinea Evangelical Student Association
Gambia	FES	Fellowship of Evangelical Students – Gambia
Ghana	GHAFES	Ghana Fellowship of Evangelical Students
Guinea-Bissau	GBU	Grupo Bíblico Universitario
Kenya	FOCUS	Fellowship of Christian Unions
Lesotho	SULTM	Scripture Union of Lesotho – Tertiary Ministry
Liberia	LIFES	Liberia Fellowship of Evangelical Students
Malawi	SCOM	Student Christian Organisation of Malawi
Mozambique	ABEMO	Aliança Bíblica Estudantil de Moçambique
Namibia	CSF	Christian Students Fellowship
Nigeria	NIFES	Nigeria Fellowship of Evangelical Students
Sierra Leone	SLEFES	Sierra Leone Fellowship of Evangelical Students
South Africa	SCO	Students' Christian Organisation
Sudan	FOCUS	Fellowship of Christian University Students
Swaziland	INCOSCM	The Inter-Collegiate Student Christian Movement

Tanzania	TAFES	Tanzania Fellowship of Evangelical Students
Uganda	FOCUS	Fellowship of Christian Unions
Zambia	ZAFES	Zambia Fellowship of Evangelical Students
Zimbabwe	FOCUS	Fellowship of Christian Unions

Francophone Africa

Benin	GBEEB	Groupes Bibliques des Elèves et Etudiants du Bénin
Burkina Faso	UGBB	Union des Groupes Bibliques du Burkina Faso
Burundi	UGBB	Union des Groupes Bibliques du Burundi
Cameroon	GBEEC	Groupes Bibliques des Elèves et Etudiants du Cameroun
Chad	UJC	Union des Jeunes Chrétiens du Tchad
Congo	GBUSC	Groupe Biblique Universitaire et Scolaire du Congo
Côte d'Ivoire	GBUCI	Groupes Bibliques Universitaires de Côte d'Ivoire
Democratic Republic of Congo	GBU	Groupes Bibliques Universitaires
Gabon	GBG	Groupes Bibliques du Gabon
Guinea Republic	GBEEG	Groupes Bibliques des Elèves et Etudiants de Guinée
Madagascar	UGBM	Union des Groupes Bibliques de Madagascar
Mali	GBEE	Groupe Biblique des Elèves et Etudiants
Mauritius	SCF	Student Christian Fellowship
Niger	GBU	Groupes Bibliques Universitaires du Niger
Rwanda	UGBR	Union des Groupes Bibliques du Rwanda
Senegal	GBUSS	Groupes Bibliques des Universitaires et Scolaires du Sénégal
Togo	GBUST	Groupes Bibliques Universitaires et Scolaires du Togo

Middle East and North Africa

Algeria	GBU	Groupes Bibliques Universitaires
Egypt	USM	University Students' Ministry
Israel	FCSI	Fellowship of Christian Students in Israel
Jordan	JUCS	Jordan University Christian Students
Lebanon	LIVF	Lebanon Inter-Varsity Fellowship
Mauritania		[Pioneering]
Morocco		
Palestinian Territory		[Pioneering]
Syria		[Pioneering]
Tunisia		

South Pacific

Australia	AFES	Australian Fellowship of Evangelical Students
Fiji	PSFC	Pacific Students for Christ
New Zealand	TSCF	Tertiary Students' Christian Fellowship
Papua New Guinea	TSCF	Tertiary Students' Christian Fellowship

East Asia

Cambodia	FES	Fellowship of Evangelical Students
Hong Kong	FES	Fellowship of Evangelical Students
Indonesia	Perkantas	Persekutuan Kristen Antar Universitas
Japan	KGK	Kirisutosha Gakusei Kai
Korea	IVF	Inter-Varsity Fellowship
Malaysia	FES	Fellowship of Evangelical Students
Mongolia	FCS	Fellowship of Christian Students
Philippines	IVCF	Inter-Varsity Christian Fellowship
Singapore	FES	Fellowship of Evangelical Students
Taiwan	CEF	Campus Evangelical Fellowship
Thailand	TCS	Thai Christian Students

South Asia

Bangladesh	BSFB	Bible Students Fellowship of Bangladesh
India	UESI	Union of Evangelical Students of India
Nepal	NBCBS	University Christian Students Fellowship of Nepal
Pakistan	PFES	Pakistan Fellowship of Evangelical Students
Sri Lanka	FOCUS	Fellowship of Christian University Students

Eurasia

Armenia	CSUA	Christian Student Union of Armenia
Azerbaijan		
Belarus		
Georgia	SKSK	Sakartvelos Kristian Studentda Kavshiri
Kazakhstan		
Kyrgyzstan		
Moldova	CSC	Comunitatea Studentilor Crestini
Russia	CCX	Soobshchestvo Studentov Kristian
Tajikistan		
Ukraine	CCX	Spivdruzhnist Studentiv Khrystyan

Central Europe

Albania	BSKSh	Besëlidhja Studentëve të Krishterë Shqiptarë
Austria	ÖSM	Österreichische Studentenmission
Bosnia	EUSFBiH	Association of Evangelical Students of Bosnia and Herzegovina
Bulgaria	BCSU	Bulgaria Christian Student Union
Croatia	STEP	Studentski Evandeoski Pokret
Cyprus		[Pioneering]
Czech Republic	UKH	Univerzitni křest'anské hnutí
Estonia	EEÜÜ	Eesti Evangeelsete Üliŏpilaste Ühendus
Greece	CESA	Christian Evangelical Students' Association

Hungary	MEKDSZ	Magyar Evangéliumi Keresztyén Diákszövetség
Latvia	LKSB	Latvijas Kristiga Studentu Braliba
Lithuania	LKSB	Lietuvos Kriksoniu Studentu Bendria
Macedonia	Exodus	Exodus
Poland	ChSA	Chrzescijanskie Stowarzyszenie Akademickie
Romania	OSCER	Organizatia Studentilor Crestini Evanghelici din România
Serbia and Montenegro	EUS	Evandeosko Udruzenje Studenata
Slovakia	VBH	Vysokoškolské Biblické Hnutie
Slovenia	ZVESh	Zveza Evangelijskih Studentov Slovenije
Turkey		[Pioneering]

Western Europe

Belgium (French-speaking)	GBU	Groupes Bibliques Universitaires
Belgium (Flemmish-speaking)	Ichtus	Ichtus
Denmark	KFS	Kristeligt Forbund for Studerende
Finland	OPKO	Suomen Evankelisluterilainen Opiskelija-ja Koululaislähetys
France	GBU	Association des Groupes Bibliques Universitaires de France
Germany	SMD	Studentenmission in Deutschland
Great Britain	UCCF	Universities and Colleges Christian Fellowship
Iceland	KSH	Kristilega Skólahreyfingin
Ireland	IFES Ireland	IFES Ireland
Italy	GBU	Gruppi Biblici Universitari
Netherlands	IFES Nederland	IFES Nederland
Norway	NKSS	Norges Kristelige Student-og Skoleungdomslag

Portugal	GBU	Grupo Bíblico Universitário de Portugal
Spain	GBU	Federación de Grupos Bíblicos Universitarios de España
Sweden	CREDO	Sveriges evangeliska student-och gymnasiströrelse
Switzerland (*French-speaking*)	GBEU	Groupes Bibliques des Ecoles et Universités
Switzerland (*German-speaking*)	VBG	Vereinigte Bibelgruppen in Schule Universität Beruf

North America

Canada (*English-speaking*)	IVCF	Inter-Varsity Christian Fellowship
Canada (*French-speaking*)	GBUC	Groupes Bibliques Universitaires et Collégiaux du Canada
USA	InterVarsity	InterVarsity Christian Fellowship

Caribbean

Antigua	ISCCF	Inter-School & Colleges Christian Fellowship
Barbados	IS/IVCF	Inter-School & Inter-Varsity Christian Fellowship
Belize	IS/IVCF	Inter-School & Inter-Varsity Christian Fellowship
French Guiana	AAGCG	L'Association des Amis du Groupe Biblique Universitaire et des Clubs Bibliques Lycéens de la Guyane
Guadeloupe	GBU	Groupes Bibliques Universitaires
Guyana	IS/IVCF	Inter-School & Inter-Varsity Christian Fellowship
Haiti	GBEUH	Groupe Biblique des Ecoles et Universités d'Haïti
Jamaica	SCF/SU	Students' Christian Fellowship & Scripture Union
Martinique	GBU	Groupes Bibliques Universitaires
St Lucia	IS/CCF	Inter-School and Colleges Christian Fellowship

Suriname	JSSM	Jesus' Students Suriname Movement
Trinidad & Tobago	IS/IVCF	Inter-School & Inter-Varsity Christian Fellowship

Latin America

Argentina	ABUA	Asociación Bíblica Universitaria Argentina
Bolivia	CCU	Comunidad Cristiana Universitaria
Brazil	ABUB	Aliança Bíblica Universitária do Brasil
Chile	GBUCH	Grupo Bíblico Universitario de Chile
Colombia	UCU	Unidad Cristiana Universitaria
Costa Rica	ECU	Estudiantes Cristianos Unidos
Cuba	Koinonia	Comunidad 'Koinonia' de Estudiantes y Profesionales Cristianos de Cuba
Dominican Republic	ADEE	Asociación Dominicana de Estudiantes Evangélicos
Ecuador	CECE	Comunidad de Estudiantes Cristianos de Ecuador
El Salvador	MUC	Movimiento Universitario Cristiano
Guatemala	GEU	Grupo Evangélico Universitario
Honduras	CCUH	Comunidad Cristiana Universitaria de Honduras
Mexico	Compa	Compañerismo Estudiantil A C
Nicaragua	CECNIC	Comunidad de Estudiantes Cristianos de Nicaragua
Panama	CEC	Comunidad de Estudiantes Cristianos
Paraguay	GBUP	Grupo Bíblico Universitario de Paraguay
Peru	AGEUP	Asociación de Grupos Evangélicos Universitarios del Perú
Puerto Rico	ABU	Asociación Bíblica Universitaria de Puerto Rico
Uruguay	CBUU	Comunidad Bíblica Universitaria de Uruguay
Venezuela	MUEVE	Movimiento Universitario Evangélico Venezolano

Notes

Foreword
1. These matters are being explored with urgency and penetration. See for instance Craig Ott and Harold A. Netland (ed.) *Globalizing Theology: Belief and Practice in an Era of World Christianity* (Grand Rapids: Baker, 2006).

Introduction: A passion for Christ's glory
1. Revelation 2:10.
2. *A Christian Critique of the University* (North Waterloo Academic Press, 1990).
3. Colossians 1:17.
4. Deuteronomy 6:5; Mark 12:30.

Chapter 1: Never underestimate what students can do
1. Ephesians 3:20.
2. Recorded by Gustav Warneck, the great historian/theologian. Much of this story appeared in David M. Howard's *Student Power in World Missions* (IVP: USA, 2nd edn, 1979).
3. The present or Renewed Moravian Church traces its roots back to Von Zinzendorf. In 1727 refugees, initially from Moravia but also from other states, were granted permission to settle on his lands in Saxony near the present-day border with Poland. The settlement was named *Herrnhut* – 'under the watch of the Lord'.
4. *The Life of God in the Soul of Man* is still available (Christian Heritage, 1995).
5. Simeon's influence was immense, and any biography of him is worth reading. He had a direct influence in forming the British and Foreign Bible Society at Cambridge in 1811 – its purpose was to make the Word of God available throughout the world in the language of the people. Many staff of IFES movements have become engaged in the ministry of what is

now the United Bible Societies (UBS). UBS has disseminated the Scriptures worldwide, and fruitful partnerships exist between its national Bible societies and IFES movements.

UCCF, the British IFES movement, traces its origins to the work begun by Charles Simeon. The Cambridge Inter-Collegiate Christian Union (CICCU) was founded in 1877. Its story is told in *From Cambridge to the World* (O. R. Barclay and R. M. Horn, IVP 2002). From its small beginnings, a national Christian Union movement was born in 1928 and it spread to other countries. The first regular meetings in Cambridge had been set up after a visit by David Livingstone, just back from Africa, 'The sort of men who are wanted for missionaries are such as I see before me,' he told the students who had gathered specially to hear him in the Senate House, 'I leave it with you.' The Cambridge University Church Missionary Union was formed in 1858. Four years later two new students came to Cambridge who had been converted in the 1859 revival. Despite the disapproval of many of the most esteemed men in the university, they formed a group of twenty students who met daily to pray. From 1867 there was also a regular daily gathering for prayer in Oxford University. Daily prayer meetings, or DPMs as they later became known, continued for over a hundred years in the life of both universities.

6. See www.martynmission.cam.ac.uk for the inspirational legacy of Henry Martyn's life. There is a moving plaque in the chancel of Holy Trinity Church, Cambridge, to his memory.

7. C. T. Studd later founded the Worldwide Evangelization Crusade (WEC).

8. Stanley Smith went on to serve in Rwanda and was a founder of the Rwanda mission.

9. David Jayakumar, UESI General Secretary, recently researched the major contribution of UESI graduates in taking the gospel to all language groups in India as well as

to many peoples beyond. There are now two hundred indigenous missions affiliated to the Indian Missions Association, many founded by UESI graduates. He concluded that perhaps as many as 50% of all India's missionaries are graduates of UESI or were closely associated with it.

10. Samuel Mills died at sea on his way back from what is now Liberia. He was thirty-five. Way beyond his time, his heart was already set on indigenous mission. He wanted to find ways of training Africans to bring the gospel to their own continent. Moved by the need for social justice, his plan was to work to repatriate African slaves whom he would teach the faith and then train in evangelism.

11. In June 1810, Mills and his fellow students made an approach to the Congregational Church Association to send them out as foreign missionaries. Later that month the first Protestant foreign missions board was formed. It enjoyed the support of numerous churches.

12. Abbreviated from Chapter 8 of David Howard's classic *Student Power in World Missions*.

13. See 1 Thessalonians 2:9.

14. See Acts 18:3–5.

15. Leah Genita serves on the IFES Executive Committee representing East Asia.

16. See note 1 below. This is the annual training course in Kiev, Ukraine. You will read more in Chapter 3.

17. To explore the possibility of giving one or two years (or more) to help to pioneer or to strengthen Christian witness among students in another country, go to www.ifesworld.org

Chapter 2: Our sovereign God and human courage

1. In 2000 a group of Eurasia staff shared prayer goals and dreams for the region. Vast distances, a post-communist heritage, difficult economies, religious opposition and headwind from state orthodoxy all created real obstacles. From this discussion the Eurasia Institute was born. By 2002

the first annual summer training programme was held in Kiev to train gifted leaders, under the direction of Bob Grahmann. The Institute has no plant but operates a distance-learning programme through the year.

2. For example Friends International (UK); ISI (USA and elsewhere); ISM (New Zealand); IMF (India).

3. Chua Wee Hian, a Chinese–Singaporean, served as the second IFES General Secretary (1972–1991). He succeeded the Australian Stacey Woods who had also been General Secretary of Inter-Varsity Canada and Intervarsity/USA.

4. Six months after Camilla-Shalom died, I learned how she had been given her name. This is the email Emmanuel and Asèle wrote. I found it very touching, so include it here with their permission.

Camilla-Shalom's life was short but she left us with a lot of good memory. I think that is why she is still very alive among us: her laughter, her calling, her games, etc. And do you know what? Her baby-sitter is still with us, although Jolly and Lewis do not need anyone to look after them. It was our way of helping her in her own healing having been the most unfortunate among us. It is so good to see the smile back on her face today.

Concerning the choice of her name: one thing our children regretted most was that they had always to leave their friends behind (Bujumbura, UK, Abidjan). At All Nations College, Jolly had a very close friend called Camilla. She was a Brazilian classmate. Her parents were there for only one year and they were very close. Both cried bitterly when they had to part. That same year, Lewis made a Dutch classmate a friend. His name was Rick. From time to time at weekends they would sleep over either at our house or at Rick's house. Rick and Camilla were greatly missed by our children.

When Shalom was about to be born, Jolly and Lewis first agreed among themselves then asked us that if the one about to come into our family was a girl, could she be called Camilla or, if a boy, could he be called Rick, in memory of these two great friends. That was why to Shalom we had to add Camilla. Her loss was a double loss, more particularly for Jolly.

As people called into the ministry of consolation, I believe it is part of God's grace and plan to have us taste what others have experienced or are experiencing.

Chapter 3: Holding out the word of life

1. David Adeney (of CIM/OMF) founded several IFES East Asian movements; David Bentley-Taylor (formerly of CIM/OMF in China and Indonesia) became UK General Secretary of Middle East Christian Outreach (MECO) and continued a fruitful writing ministry; David Penman was later Archbishop of Melbourne; Gottfried Osei-Mensah was appointed first International Director of the Lausanne movement; David Gitari became Bishop of Nairobi, then Archbishop of Kenya; Alistair Kennedy served as Vice-President of WEC International; and John White practised as a Christian psychiatrist, and wrote several best-selling IVP titles.

2. Ziel Machado, IFES Regional Secretary, traces the benefit in the region over the next fifteen years: 'National movements found a way to adapt the experience. Even now many movements are using principles from Cochabamba 91.'

3. Prof. Nigel M. de S. Cameron was active in the British IFES movement (UCCF) while a student in Cambridge and Edinburgh, and served as national student chairman of the UK Theological Students Fellowship (now RTSF). Formerly Provost at Trinity International University, he is now President of the Institute on Biotechnology and the Human Future and Research Professor of Bioethics, Illinois Institute of Technology, USA.

4. 'What are Christian Apologetics?' in *Evangelicals Now*, November 2005 (www.e-n.org.uk).

5. Daniel Bourdanné has edited a unique book written out of the Great Lakes crucible, bringing first-hand accounts of how students and graduates of the IFES movements responded during the genocide. It addresses profound questions of tribalism and humanity and brings perceptive insights on human identity from the early chapters of Genesis. *Tribalisme en Afrique* (ed.) Daniel Bourdanné with Antoine Rutayisiré, Emmanuel Ndikumana and Abel Ndjerareou. Press Bibliques Africaines (ISBN 2–911752–28–7).

Chapter 4: Students and world mission

1. I have told Adoniram Judson's story in brief in Chapter 8. Anything written by or about Mildred Cable, Jonathan Goforth – or more recently Helen Roseveare, David Adeney, David Bentley-Taylor, Leslie Lyall and Michael Griffiths is worth reading. The list could go on and on – men and women whose faith has been nurtured in their student fellowship and who have dedicated their lives to cross-cultural mission.

2. John Stott has contributed a masterly four-minute overview of how mission is integral to authentic biblical Christianity in Robin Wells's distinctive book *Jesus Says Go* (Monarch/Kregel, 2006). A voice file is hosted on the UCCF website and available for use in meetings or training events as a free download at www.uccf.org.uk/omt. For a fuller treatment see Chapter 19 of John Stott's *The Contemporary Christian* (IVP, 1995) or Rose Dowsett's *God's Missionary Heart: From Eden to Eternity* which forms Part 2 of *Jesus Says Go*.

3. As described by Sir Geoffrey Elton, Emeritus Professor of Modern History at Cambridge University.

4. In 1800 the Bible was available in only seventy languages. Today we have Scripture in over 2,200 of the world's 6,500 languages and 80% of people have access to it in a language

they can understand. From 1960 to 2000 the number of Western evangelicals grew from 57 million to about 100 million; non-Western evangelicals grew from twenty-nine million to over 220 million. The church has become truly global.

Of the 279 mega-languages in the world (at least one million speakers), only ninety-one languages still lack gospel witness by radio, and between ten to fifteen languages are added annually. It is salutary to note that each year there are some 25,000 new Christian books published and 68 million Bibles distributed. There is enough evangelism going on to evangelize the world 79 times over – if it were distributed evenly.

5. Langham Partnership International (LPI) was founded by John Stott to address these needs. Its directors are all graduates of IFES national movements, and LPI works closely with IFES staff in its training seminars. Jonathan Lamb, Director of Preaching, served as IFES Associate General Secretary.

6. The publishing house in Francophone Africa now serves twenty countries.

7. I quote a paper prepared by Las Newman, IFES Associate General Secretary, 2003. 'The term Integral Mission, or *Misión Integral* in Spanish, originated in the mission discourses of the Micah Network. This is a network of Evangelical Relief and Development practitioners of which IFES statesman C. René Padilla is a founding father. The Micah Declaration on Integral Mission (2001) states that "Integral mission or holistic transformation is the proclamation and demonstration of the gospel." The Declaration states that social involvement and proclamation are not just to be done alongside each other, but to be integrally related. As in the life of Jesus, so in *Misión Integral*, being, doing and saying are at the heart of our integral task.'

Chapter 5: Making a difference in society

1. This quotation, while commonly attributed to Edmund Burke, the nineteenth-century British statesman, has never actually been sourced in his writings. But that does not take away from its perceptive quality.
2. For more on Tony Wilmot's remarkable life, see obituaries in *The Times* 27 December 1996; *The Telegraph* 28 December 1996; *The Oxford Dictionary of National Biography*. Eve Wilmot, who died in 2006, was the daughter of Algernon Stanley-Smith of the Rwanda Mission and grand-daughter of Peregrine Stanley-Smith, one of the Cambridge Seven. She and Tony were widely known as 'Auntie and Uncle' or as 'Mummy and Daddy' to thousands of African students. We honour them for their deeply sacrificial commitment to building Christ's church in the universities across that continent.
3. Thomas Aquinas (1225–1274) *Summa Theologica* (Part 2: Section 1; Q. 114 Article 1 'Whether a man may merit anything from God?' Objection 3).
4. If you are exploring the possibility of Christian ministry, I commend Ajith Fernando's searching booklet *An Authentic Servant*.
5. Harry Blamires *The Christian Mind* (Ann Arbor, 1963); John Stott, *Your Mind Matters* (InterVarsity Press, 1973). Both still available in new editions.

Chapter 6: The reconciling power of the gospel

1. See the story of Samuel subduing the Philistines at Mizpah in 1 Samuel 7:7–13.
2. This reading plan, which takes people through the whole Bible once and the New Testament and Psalms twice in a year has been used by countless Christians around the world. It was devised by a Scottish pastor, Robert Murray McCheyne (1813–1843). A new edition has been published by IFES.

3. Roger Bowen of the Church Mission Society (CMS) offered his reflections on the Rwanda holocaust in the 1995 J. C. Jones Memorial Lecture. Available from CMS through www.cms-uk.org

Chapter 7: The new Europe since 1989

1. Vladimir Martinovsky, a courageous believer, had helped to lead the communion service at the 1939 International Conference of Evangelical Students, held in Cambridge, UK (see Chapter 10). This was the forerunner of the Harvard conference at which IFES was founded after the war.
2. It was then very unusual for any known evangelical who was not from abroad to be allowed to complete a degree in most parts of the USSR, so sharing friendship with Christians from overseas was not easy.
3. CCX is in Cyrillic script and pronounced SS-Ah.
4. There were three main religious groupings: Serbian Orthodox, Croatian Catholic and Bosnian Muslim. Tito had established a delicate balance of power with top jobs constantly rotating among the different ethnic groups. Each Republic was responsible for its own internal affairs, while the Yugoslav government took care of such matters as defence and foreign policy. The system started to fail after Tito's death. No leader was able to unite the different interests: the economy began to deteriorate and the richer Republics resented having to prop up the economies of the poorer ones. Slobodan Milosovic's espousal of the Serbian cause made tensions worse.

   In 1991 Slovenia and Croatia both declared independence. Serbia and the Yugoslav army wanted to keep Yugoslavia intact, and tried to reverse these decisions forcibly; the inevitable result was civil war: a brief one in Slovenia, and a longer and bloodier one in Croatia. In September 1992 Bosnia held its own referendum – again the majority voted for independence but Bosnia would have problems in

making this work. The west of the country was largely
Croat but the east mainly Serb, and the Bosnian Serbs had
boycotted the vote entirely. So Bosnia's declaration of
independence again resulted in civil war. The fighting was
ended by international intervention and Serbia was forced to
accept that the former Yugoslavia had now shrunk to two
areas: Serbia and Montenegro, Macedonia having also
seceded. Trouble in Kosova between the majority Albanian
population and the minority Serbs had been endemic even
in Tito's time. The Kosova Albanians wanted independence
from Serbia, but Kosova – the scene of the great battle
against the Ottoman Turks – is hallowed ground to Serbia
and they would not willingly give it up.

Chapter 8: The call to sacrifice

1. IVP UK published his autobiography *An Adopted Son* (1985)
   which is worth looking out for second-hand.

Chapter 9: Providence and perseverance

1. Kornél Herjeczki serves on the International Executive
   Committee as one of the representatives from Europe/Eurasia.
2. *The Independent* 14 May 2005; *The Times* 25 May 2005. *The
   Independent* traced the specific influence of IVP on
   theological publishing, which is a story to tell in itself.
   I quote briefly from *The Times*:

> Such leading writers as John Stott, J. I. Packer and the
> philosopher Francis Schaeffer were launched by Inchley. He
> took pleasure in nurturing the skills of new writers, would take
> them on walks to find out what they wanted to tackle, and then
> hound them to deliver the goods.
>
> IVP's authors, drawn from academia, the Church, industry,
> medicine and ethics, have included some of the sharpest minds
> in evangelicalism. Almost all, like Inchley himself, became
> established in their faith through their university Christian Union.

Chapter 10: Looking ahead

1. Tony Lambert's *China's Christian Millions* (OMF/Monarch 1997, 2006) gives a good overview of what is happening among Chinese intellectuals.
2. *Operation World* is updated in book form regularly and available from any Christian bookshop or online bookseller. It can be viewed at www.operationworld.org
3. For more on SAT-7's ministry see www.sat7.com
4. Volume 2, issue 5.

Appendix 1: What *distinctive* contribution has IFES brought to the global church?

1. This first appeared in 1936 and it is still in print, revised to address successive new generations.

Appendix 3: How to pray for students

1. This text is available in leaflet form. Orders (no charge) to info@ifesworld.org or write to the IFES International Office at 321 Banbury Road, Oxford OX2 7JZ, UK.

Appendix 4: IFES national movements

1. The names of some countries/movements have been omitted for reasons of security.

Recommended reading

Out of the Saltshaker by Rebecca Manley Pippert (IVP) – a classic
on personal evangelism.

Jesus Says Go by Robin Wells (Monarch/Kregel with IFES/
OMF/SIM) – for anyone exploring short-term or long-term
cross-cultural mission.

A Time for Mission by Samuel Escobar (IVP/LPI) – a stimulating
analysis of global mission today.

From Cambridge to the World by O. R. Barclay and R. M. Horn
(IVP) – principles from the early days of the CICCU traced
through to 2002.

The Grace of Giving by John Stott (IFES/LPI booklet) – ten
principles of Christian giving from 2 Corinthians 8 – 9.

More Precious than Gold, McCheyne Bible Reading Plan (IFES
booklet) – a plan taking its users through the whole Bible in
one or two years.

An Authentic Servant by Ajith Fernando (IFES/OMF booklet) –
a searching read for leaders in churches, student groups or
mission agencies.

Jesus-Driven Ministry by Ajith Fernando (IVP).

Ultimate Realities by R. M. Horn (IVP) – an explanation of the
UCCF doctrinal basis.